LOST
HAMMOND
INDIANA

LOST
HAMMOND
INDIANA

JOSEPH S. PETE

Published by The History Press
Charleston, SC
www.historypress.com

Copyright © 2020 by Joseph S. Pete
All rights reserved

First published 2020

Manufactured in the United States

ISBN 9781467142861

Library of Congress Control Number: 2019956022

Notice: The information in this book is true and complete to the best of our knowledge. It is offered without guarantee on the part of the author or The History Press. The author and The History Press disclaim all liability in connection with the use of this book.

All rights reserved. No part of this book may be reproduced or transmitted in any form whatsoever without prior written permission from the publisher except in the case of brief quotations embodied in critical articles and reviews.

To my wife, Meredith: my sun, my moon and my starry, scintillating sky.

CONTENTS

Acknowledgements 9
Introduction 11

1. State Line Slaughterhouse and Early Days 27
2. Ice Harvest at Wolf Lake 35
3. Roby 41
4. West Hammond 48
5. Five Points 52
6. Downtown 66
7. Movie Theaters 77
8. Department Stores 90
9. Jean Shepherd's Hammond 102
10. Hotels 105
11. Restaurants 110
12. Trains 120
13. Standard Steel Car Company/Pullman-Standard Factory 122
14. Taylor Chain Company 127
15. W.B. Conkey/Rand McNally Plant 129
16. Sears Roebuck/Alvah Roebuck 138
17. Straube Piano Company 143
18. State Line Generating Plant 146
19. Nine Span Bridge 149
20. WJOB and *The Hammond Times* 152

Contents

21. Woodmar Country Club	157
22. Woodmar Mall	160
23. Hammond Pros and Other Professional Sports	166
24. Hammond Distilling Company	174
25. Bank Calumet and Other Financial Institutions	179
26. Indiana Botanic Gardens	183
27. The Roller Dome	187
28. John Dillinger Museum	189
Epilogue	193
Bibliography	199
Index	201
About the Author	205

ACKNOWLEDGEMENTS

The author would like to thank the assistance of the Hammond Public Library's Suzanne G. Long Local History Room, the Hammond Historical Society, the Calumet Regional Archives at Indiana University Northwest, the Hammond High School Class of 1959 history website, the archives of *The Times of Northwest Indiana* and the *Post-Tribune*, his parents and family, Mr. Klora and other teachers, iced coffee, LCD Soundsystem's "Losing My Edge" and other songs he played on repeat while writing, the "there ain't no laws while you're drinking Claws" guy and the secret splendor that lurks within everyone, however well hidden.

INTRODUCTION

Northwest Indiana is one of the most heavily industrialized places on Earth with all its steel mills, oil refineries and ports, and Hammond is one of the biggest hubs of industry there. Though overshadowed by its next-door neighbor Chicago and perhaps not as well known as the adjacent Steel City, Gary, Indiana, Hammond has given the wider world soap, books, tanks, gasoline, corn syrup, horse food, processed hogs and lots and lots of hearty midwestern beef. The city has made trains, chains, cigars, shirts, candy, nuts, player pianos, commercial wallpaper, concrete roof slabs, gutters, boilers, potato digging devices, screws and many steel products. Needless to say, Hammond is a city that makes stuff. It's a city of hulking factories and rumbling railroads that takes pride in its industriousness. It's suffered from some of the corresponding environmental problems and even had a river catch fire like the Cuyahoga River in Cleveland. But there's far more to Hammond than just manufacturing and blue-collar workers. Hammond was home to one of the first National Football League teams and early National Basketball Association teams. It gestated *A Christmas Story* author Jean Shepherd, the legendary professional wrestler Terry Funk and Sears co-founder Alvah Curtis Roebuck. Once a major retail and entertainment hub, Hammond had many treasured landmarks like the Phil Smidt's perch palace, Goldblatt's, the E.C. Minas Department Store, the Paramount and Parthenon theaters, the Woodmar Mall, Madura's Danceland and all the bright lights and beckoning attractions at Five Points. While the marquee lights have dimmed at the grand movie palaces and the

Introduction

As this vintage promotional brochure shows, Hammond is home to many recreational activities like sailing on Wolf Lake. *Calumet Regional Archives.*

elegant department stores have faded into fond memories, the city remains home to universities, fine dining, casino gaming, festivals, massive outdoor concerts, beaches and some magnificent pockets of nature like Wolf Lake, which *Men's Journal* named the best place in the country for windsurfing.

In 1847, immigrants from Germany, East Prussia and Wales settled on the southern shore of Lake Michigan near what is now Hammond. They quickly discovered the land was unsuitable for cash crops like corn, wheat and soybeans that dominated the largely agricultural landscape downstate, though their gardens still sprouted blackberries, strawberries, huckleberries and other sweet fruit. The German language was spoken around town in the city's early days. The first settlers farmed, worked on railroads, guided people to Chicago and hunted, bagging as many as one hundred ducks in a day. The nineteenth-century historian Alfred Andreas described the city as an "unbroken forest of heavy timber, but which has long since disappeared under the aggressive civilization of the white man's ax." The Region was one of the last places to be settled in Indiana because it was so inhospitable. The area along the lakeshore of Lake Michigan was described by Andreas as a wilderness "with swamps, marshes, quaking bogs, and invincible sandhills." "During part of the year, the immense swamps between Lake Michigan and the Grand Calumet River and between the latter and the Little Calumet became seas, dammed by fallen timber and matted leaves," according to the Federal Writers' Project's *The Calumet Region Historical Guide*. The guide continues: "On the shore of Lake Michigan, sandhills some 200 feet high, with bases of 300 to 400 feet, offered no attraction to the pioneer home-seeker. Quaking bogs and tamarack swamps, around which the Indian routed his path, made other areas impenetrable to the inexperienced settlers." Ernst and Caroline Hohman established Hohman's Tavern and a toll bridge across the Calumet River near the state line in 1851. John Shedd, the second president and chairman of Marshall Field's and the namesake of the Shedd Aquarium, who owned a lot of property in the Hammond area, reportedly would chance it by crossing the ice in the winter so he would not have to pay the toll.

From the start, Hammond was the little brother to neighboring Chicago, the "meatpacker of the world," which shaped its early development. George Hammond and Marcus Towle established a slaughterhouse and beef packaging plant just across the state line in Hammond in 1869. It was

Hammond Dairy Company was one of the city's early businesses. *Hammond Public Library.*

Introduction

Hammond's first industrial enterprise, grew into a major supplier of meat across the Midwest and paved the way for Hammond to be incorporated as a city a few years later. The meatpacking plant was so prominent Hammond was first known as "State Line Slaughterhouse," according to T.H. Ball's *A History of Northwestern Indiana from 1800–1900*. It was not until a post office opened in the city that it was given the far less descriptive name of Hammond. The legend goes that George Hammond's brother "Honest Tom" Hammond had a coin flip with co-founder Towle; the winner would have the city named after his family, and the loser would get a main road named after his. Tom Hammond, of course, won. He went on to become mayor and was instrumental in bringing the W.B. Conkey bookbinding factory to town. But he was nowhere near as central to the city's development as his brother George, a Massachusetts native who started out making leather pocketbooks after dropping out of school at the age of ten and ended up working in different mattress factories. George Hammond spent most of his life in Detroit, where he established a meat market that grew into a large retail and wholesale meat store, but nonetheless made much of his fortune in the city southeast of Chicago on the shores of Lake Michigan that would eventually bear his name. His thirty-acre meatpacking operation at Hohman Avenue and Willow Court just north of downtown Hammond was the city's earliest economic engine, grew successful enough to have a sister facility in South Omaha, Nebraska, and eventually shut down after a fire in 1901 that left nearly two thousand workers out of a job.

In its last year in operation, the G.H. Hammond Company slaughtered 350,000 cattle, 350,000 pigs and 400,000 sheep in Hammond. It helped feed the voracious demand for western beef back east with the pioneering innovation of the refrigerated railcar, which proved to be far more efficient than the earlier technique of dumping ice on dead cows, which discolored the meat, or shipping live cattle that only wasted away during the long, slow journey of about thirty-five miles per hour. The slaughterhouse helped drive Hammond's greatest population surge of 128 percent between 1890 and 1900, but the rapidly expanding city still grew by more than 70 percent in each of the next three decades. In those heady early days of giddy growth, Hammond rivaled Crown Point, squabbling over whether it should instead be the seat of the county government. Hammond lost that fight but ended up with both a federal court and Lake County Superior Courts, which has made downtown a longtime hub for law firms and legal offices. "By 1890 Hammond was Lake County's largest community with a population of 5,428," Kenneth J. Schoon wrote in his book *Calumet Beginnings*. "St.

INTRODUCTION

Since its inception, Hammond has been home to many industrial businesses like Hammond Cornice Works. *Hammond Public Library.*

Margaret's Hospital, the first hospital in the northern Calumet Area, opened in 1898. That same year, W.B. Conkey built the world's largest printing and bookbinding plant. By 1900, with numerous industries, two banks, fourteen churches, one synagogue, and a waterworks providing Lake Michigan water, the population topped 12,000." Gary eclipsed Hammond as the largest city in the Calumet Region by 1920, but Hammond took the title back in 2010 after decades of population loss in the neighboring Steel City, which has suffered from blight, crime and scorched-earth suburban abandonment. Hammond has retained that title ever since.

Stretching over nearly twenty-five square miles right on the state line, Hammond borders Gary, East Chicago, Whiting, Munster, Highland and Griffith in Indiana and Burnham, Calumet City, Chicago and Lansing over in Illinois. Though down from its height of a population of 111,698 in 1960 and far from its presumed peak population of up to 130,000 if it were "full up," Hammond is now the largest city in Lake County, the second-most populous county in Indiana after Marion County, the home to Indianapolis, and is one of the most populous suburban counties in the Chicago metropolitan area, according to the U.S. Census Bureau. *The Times of Northwest Indiana*, once *The Hammond Times*, the source of much of the

Introduction

LaSalle Steel, now Niagra LaSalle Corporation, is one of Hammond's many factories. *Hammond Public Library.*

information in this book, is also the fourth-largest daily newspaper in the Chicago metro area after the *Chicago Tribune*, the *Chicago Sun-Times* and the largely suburban *Daily Herald*.

The first Northwest Indiana city to see significant industrial development, Hammond has long been a center of the manufacturing heft of the Calumet Region that was once known as the "Workshop for the World." Hammond's identity and reputation long have been tied up with the Region and its neighboring cities in North Lake County: Gary, East Chicago and Whiting. Though the Calumet Region technically stretches from South Side Chicago through the southeastern suburbs and Northwest Indiana east to the Michigan state line, many purists describe the old industrial cities as the real Region. "Calumet's four cities, geographically and industrially, form a unit," according to *The Calumet Region Historical Guide*. "They merge into each other so completely that a tourist frequently passes from Gary to Hammond or to East Chicago, unaware that he has entered another city. In many ways that are bound to one another."

Introduction

It's blue-collar to the core.

Hard work, often at factories with smokestacks, is forged in the city's DNA. "A majority of the 260,000 inhabitants of the four Calumet cities belong to the industrial working class," according to *The Calumet Region Historical Guide*, which was published in 1939. "These workers, whether they are members of independent unions, craft-unions, or vertical unions, represent the most important factor in the whole industrial process—labor. Their aims are identical: 'right treatment at the shop,' 'fair wages and hours,' 'improved working conditions' and the establishment of what they consider the democratic rights in industry: 'collective bargaining, security, etcetera.'" Hammond also has been an ethnically diverse city from the start. Neighboring East Chicago was once home to more than ninety-nine dialects from across the world, and Hammond was settled by many eastern Europeans who had first immigrated to Cleveland. "To this day, or at least a day before this day, the north side of Whiting is predominately Slovak and the beautiful cathedral in Robertsdale (technically Hammond), is so Slovak that, when it was begun, the congregation sent to the old country for a priest," Region historian Archibald McKinlay wrote in his *Times of Northwest Indiana* column in 2013. "These Slavic-speaking newcomers retained their homeland languages and that concept spread to other ethnic groups." Though a lunch-pail city situated in the cheaper and more working-class Indiana, Hammond has suffered from many of the same setbacks as overall Chicagoland, such as heavy traffic. "Indianapolis Boulevard had the 'biggest Sunday traffic of any one street in the world,'" according to the *Hammond, Indiana Bicentennial Yearbook*. "There were no alternate routes to the east as now. When repairs were necessary, the traffic flow was the nearest thing to chaos and anarchy in the history of Hammond."

While some of its neighboring cities are defined by their hulking steel mills and sprawling oil refineries, Hammond always supported many different enterprises instead of a few giants. The city is home to oil tanks, warehouses, railroad marshaling yards and a variety of manufacturing enterprises like the steel service center Berlin Metals, Cargill, American Steel Foundries, Amsted Rail and Jupiter Aluminum. Hammond has lost factories, jobs and residents over the years but did not suffer as much as neighboring Rust Belt cities like Gary and East Chicago during the 1970s and 1980s because its economy was more diversified. Hammond has been home to a variety of industries that included construction, transportation, banking, health care, and hospitality. The city encompasses many hotels off Indiana Toll Road and the Borman Expressway, as well as the South Shore Convention and

Above: Manufacturers like LaSalle Steel have long made up Hammond's industrial backbone. *Hammond Public Library.*

Left: Hammond has been home to companies like Allied Structural Steel, which supplied metal for the I-35 bridge in Minneapolis that collapsed in 2007, killing thirteen. *Hammond Public Library.*

Introduction

Visitors Center's architecturally distinguished Indiana Welcome Center that's the hub of tourism in the Region.

Hammond retains neighborhoods that rival any suburbs, such as the mansions along Hohman Avenue. It's a college town that's home to both Purdue University Northwest and Calumet College of St. Joseph. Heavy industry like BP Whiting Refinery silos coexists with resplendent nature such as the rippling surface of Wolf Lake, the leafy canopies of Gibson Woods and the majestic shoreline of Lake Michigan. There's art to nourish the soul in the W.F. Wellman Exhibition Hall and statewide theater premieres with Chicago actors at the Towle Theatre. Not just a destination for Chicagoans seeking cheap gas and cheaper smokes, there's antique shopping downtown, zombie bar crawls in Hessville and one thing everyone can agree on, regardless of political beliefs, doctrines or worldviews: the widely celebrated queso fundido at the dining institution El Taco Real.

Home to the very active Hammond Historical Society, Hammond has been a city that respects and preserves its history: Take the Little Red School House. Every school in the Region used to send kids to the Little Red School House in Hessville, a historical site that dramatized how education happened in the city's early pioneer days. The Little Red School House was built in 1869 as the Joseph Hess School and was one of the oldest buildings constructed in Hammond, according to *Panorama Now* magazine. Hess, a merchant, postmaster and the first North Township trustee, was the namesake of Hessville, which he founded in 1852 and that was annexed by the City of Hammond in 1923, prompting East Chicago to unsuccessfully attempt to annex the entire city of Hammond. Hess was the first to settle the area by 169th Street and Kennedy Avenue in southeast Hammond. The old-school schoolhouse at 7205 Kennedy Avenue in Hammond was built with limestone and later clay from the Little Calumet River, as well as stone from the Thornton Quarry, the "Midwest's Grand Canyon," just across the state line in Illinois. Cheaper brick was used the complete the upper portion of the iconic building, which closed just before the dawn of the twentieth century though the exact year is in dispute. Originally located where the U.S. Post Office is today, the Little Red Schoolhouse was moved to a prominent spot in Hessville Park on Kennedy Avenue in 1971.

"Although no longer used as a school after 1896, the building remained a focal point for the community, serving as headquarters for William Jennings Bryan's 1896 presidential campaign, a dance hall, a place of worship, a funeral parlor, a community meeting hall and a private residence," according to *Panorama Now*. "The Hessville Historical Society purchased the

INTRODUCTION

The Little Red School House was built in 1869 for early pioneers. *Hammond Public Library.*

Hessville Historical Society Volunteers renovated the pioneer-era Little Red School House in 1971. *Hammond Public Library.*

INTRODUCTION

The Little Red School House was moved to its current location in Hessville Park in 1971. *Hammond Public Library.*

sturdy building in 1971 for a mere dollar and The Little Red Schoolhouse reopened as a museum and community center." It still stands sentry along the main drag in Hammond's Hessville neighborhood. "The Little Red Schoolhouse will long become a tangible glimpse into Hammond's past for all the residents of Hammond, Lake County and even Indiana as a whole, since plans are in the offing to promote the unique building," added the *Hammond, Indiana American Bicentennial Yearbook*. "Oddly enough, the Little Red Schoolhouse closed its doors in 1897, the same year that school attendance became compulsory in Indiana."

Many longtime Hammond institutions have departed. Some had a fateful date with the wrecking ball. Others left behind space that had to be radically reinvented after the bygone world that birthed them passed on, like the Little Red School House or P.H. Mueller & Sons Inc. Since the nineteenth century, Mueller & Sons had been a hardware store and an anchor of downtown Hammond, the hub of commerce at Hohman and Sibley. "Mueller's Hardware Store, in business since 1887, has been at its location at 416 Sibley Street since 1902," Kenneth J. Schoon wrote in *Calumet Beginnings*. "The original tin ceiling was made within the building." The hardware store helped Hammond homeowners with their

Introduction

Civil War reenactors helped celebrate the Hammond's bicentennial celebration at the Little Red School House in 1976. *Hammond Public Library.*

maintenance projects for more than a century but saw sales decline as customers decamped to the suburbs and retail shifted away from downtown. Dave Mueller, a wayward beatnik son, returned after a long stint finding his bliss out on the West Coast to save the family business, despite the forlorn and even decrepit condition of much of the rest of downtown Hammond. With the hardware business struggling, he transformed his family's longtime home improvement store into an art gallery, a vintage one where it still looks like customers could get keys made or sort through loose nuts and bolts. He's exhibited the work of artists Charles Rowling, Lou Shields and Jim Siergey, whose underground "Cultural Jet Lag" cartoons have appeared in *Time* magazine and alternative weeklies across the country, and hosted open mic nights on Thursday, which drew musicians and artistically inclined types from throughout the Region. You can go to the Paul Henry's Art Gallery to hear acoustic singer-songwriters, jazz, big band bands and even punk. "Generations of older Region residents knew it not as an art gallery but as P.H. Mueller & Sons, Inc., one of the city's oldest businesses," Meredith Colias-Pete wrote in the *Post-Tribune*. "Once a month, the Northwest Indiana and Chicago punk scene has found an

INTRODUCTION

The Little Red School House has been used to show students what education was like back in the nineteenth century. *Hammond Public Library.*

unlikely home at Paul Henry's Art Gallery in Hammond where nearly 50 teens and 20-somethings come to see shows for under $10."

Though many historical landmarks have vanished or been completely repurposed and the city is not entirely devoid of urban problems, Hammond has avoided the stark decline of neighboring cities and much of the Rust Belt. It's nowhere near as besieged by blight, crime, gangs, depopulation and the depreciation of property values as neighboring Gary, East Chicago

Left: The longtime hardware store Paul Henry's saved itself by becoming an art gallery. *Photo by author.*

Below: An artist paints a mural by Paul Henry's in downtown Hammond. *Photo by author.*

Introduction

or Calumet City. It's a city still looking toward the future, with a widely imitated College Bound program that sends local high school graduates off to state universities, a growing water utility serving Chicago's south suburbs, a forthcoming expansion of the South Shore Line and economic development efforts like the state-of-the-art Hammond SportsPlex to draw in more youth sports travel teams. Old companies that built up the city like the Hammond Buggy Company, People's Coal and Ice, the Chicago Safe and Lock Company, the Ax Factory, Nail Company and Western Rawhide Company may be long gone, but Hammond remains a city with both a storied past and reason for optimism about the future.

As Twitter humorist Region Rat Rants puts it, it's "the best city near Chicago that starts with the letter H."

1
STATE LINE SLAUGHTERHOUSE AND EARLY DAYS

For all intents and purposes, Hammond started in the nineteenth century as a slaughterhouse that killed the cattle that grazed out west, processed the carcasses and sent the meat back to the East Coast, where most of the country's population was still centered. The city was first officially known as State Line Slaughterhouse in 1872 because that's all Hammond originally was, save for a few random settlers. Excluding settlements like Hessville that would later be annexed into the city, all that occupied the land that constitutes the modern-day city was one store, a boardinghouse for the slaughterhouse workers and the G.H. Hammond Meat Company, the only industry in town. The G.H. Hammond Meat Company operated for more than thirty years during one of the most rapid periods of growth in Hammond history, where the city shot up from a few hundred residents to more than twelve thousand. The slaughterhouse was so central to Hammond's early identity that the community's main social event in the early years was the Butchers' Picnic at Drackerts Grove in which men in leather aprons congregated with dressing knives sheathed in their belts. The skilled butchers competed to see who could dress a row of steers fastest.

The meatpacking plant south of the Grand Calumet River between Hohman Avenue and the Illinois state line sent beef, lamb and other meats on refrigerated cars cooled off with ice from Wolf Lake to New York City and other East Coast destinations. The *Boston Daily Advertiser* marveled at how cold and dry the first shipment of beef was, noting how "the meat was in better condition than that received directly from our home markets."

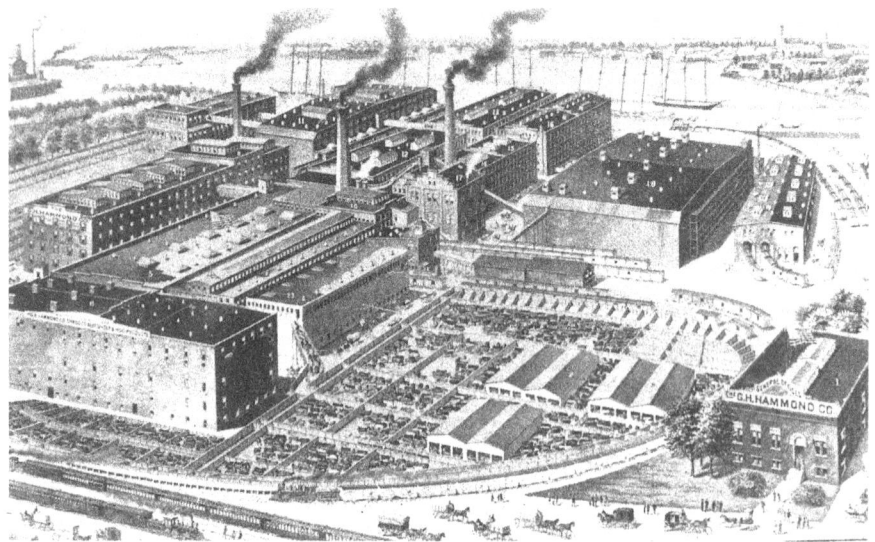

The G.H. Hammond Meat Company slaughterhouse played an integral role in the city's development. *Hammond Public Library.*

At that time in America, most meat traveled at least one thousand miles before reaching the dinner plate. About two-thirds of the meat was raised west of the Mississippi River, but about two-thirds of that was consumed east of the Mississippi. Shipments of beef from Detroit businessman George Hammond's plant eventually traveled all the way to Europe, which became one of the State Line Slaughterhouse's main markets, according to the Hammond High School Class of 1959 local history website. In ads during the 1890s, the G.H. Hammond Meat Company's slaughterhouse promised meats and lard, touting dressed beef, corned beef, roast beef, tongue, mutton, canned meat, potted ham, deviled ham and breakfast sausage that was "mild in cure (not salty.)" In the early years, the business employed eighteen men who shipped off three or four train carloads of cattle a day, according to T.H. Ball's *Northwestern Indiana from 1800 through 1900.*

By 1884, the slaughterhouse butchered three thousand heads of cattle a week. "Five to six hundred cattle are slaughtered here daily, while the full capacity of the houses is double these figures," A.T. Andreas wrote in *A History of Hammond* in 1884. "The monthly expenses for stock reach the sum of $1,350,000, while their monthly payroll amounts to over $20,000. The company is engaged almost exclusively in what is known as the dressed beef traffic, employing a great number of refrigerator cars to transport their meats to Eastern markets. Connected with the packing houses and operated by the same company is an extensive oleomargarine oil factory which turns out daily forty tierces of oil." Growth was rapid. The plant "boomed beyond all comprehension" with business doubling from $1 million in 1873 to $2 million a year in 1875. "Now in 1900, from five thousand to six thousand head of cattle and an equal number of hogs and put into shape for shipment each week," Ball wrote. "Number of persons employed 1,400." At the time, most of the workers hailed from Germany or Austria, according to *The Times of Northwest Indiana*. Two out of Hammond's three churches were German.

It was all made possible with technological innovation that was revolutionary for its time. Railroad cars were lined with horsehair and packed with broken ice and salt to keep the meat refrigerated and fresh. "A man by the name of William Davis in Detroit, a merchant near Hammond, had been shipping fish and even fruit to the east in the late 1860s by railroad and Hammond got him to design the first refrigerator car for meat," according to the *Hammond, Indiana American Bicentennial Yearbook*. "The car had ice placed in narrow chambers at each side of the car, opening only from the top to the outside. The ice was thus not directly in contact with the meat and the air over the meat was both dry and cold."

Workers at the G.H. Hammond Meat Company slaughterhouse often did not stay long because of the lack of lodging in town. *Hammond Public Library.*

But Davis died before the first shipment of beef made it to Boston, and George Hammond took over the business.

He ended up locating it in Hammond because he was looking for somewhere close to the thriving cattle market in Chicago's Union Stock Yards and a reliable source of ice. George Hammond bought fifteen acres of land along the Grand Calumet River on the Indiana-Illinois state line and the Michigan Central Railroad and built a $6,000 wooden packinghouse there in 1869. Carpenters from Chicago and Detroit raised it with lumber that was unloaded from three train cars in an unscheduled but fateful stop that would bring industry to the Calumet Region. Marcus Towle, a butcher from New Hampshire who put in one-sixth of the initial capital into G.H. Hammond Meat Company, became manager of the slaughterhouse. The facility started slaughtering cattle at 4:00 a.m. every day and would dress and process the meat until about 7:00 p.m. Workers did not get holidays off, and Towle, who later launched many ventures in town, himself often worked on the books until 10:00 p.m. They eventually got the Sabbath off at the insistence of a financier from back east who had religious qualms about such a grinding workload. "It took stamina and iron will to run such an operation for it was a 7-day per week run, with no time nor days off for anyone," noted the *Hammond, Indiana American Bicentennial Yearbook*. "It was about 1878, however, when they were in need of future financing, that they were cut back to six days a week. A banker in Boston, a Mr. Bradford who termed himself a Christian, was horrified at the demands on the men and 'refused to sell the souls of men for money' unless the situation was rectified. After almost 10 years of such work everyone was willing to capitulate."

Slaughtering 100,000 heads of cattle a year, producing 50,000 pounds of oleomargarine a day and shipping the end products with 800 train cars at its height, the G.H. Hammond Meat Company transformed an area that had been avoided by pioneer families because of its marshes, formidable sand ridges, hostile winters and the scalding wind chill off Lake Michigan. The slaughterhouse's animating presence spawned other industries like retail stores, a skating rink, the distillery, a lumberyard and a wharf that unloaded schooners from South Chicago. The accompanying population growth spawned three churches of the Catholic, Lutheran and Methodist Episcopal variety. Hammond only continued to grow. Much like Judge Elbert Gary and his neighboring namesake city of Gary, George Hammond would spend little time in the city that eventually bore his name. He continued to live in Detroit, where he was the largest owner of real estate at the time. George Hammond was in fact the namesake of Detroit's first skyscraper, the

The G.H. Hammond Meat Company slaughterhouse was the city's first major employer. *Hammond Public Library.*

151-foot Hammond Building, which was erected across from Detroit City Hall in downtown Detroit in 1889. As he amassed wealth and real estate interests, George Hammond wanted to expand his meatpacking empire and started looking to set up another slaughterhouse in Omaha in 1885. But he died before he could complete that project. "Tragically enough, he pressed himself too hard and suddenly died in 1886 at the age of 48," according to the *Hammond, Indiana American Bicentennial Yearbook*. "For years he had been continually on the move. He once remarked that he usually spent 200 nights out each year aboard Pullman Cars and an ordinary bed no longer enabled him to get a good night's rest."

Ironically perhaps, George Hammond long resisted the idea of incorporating State Line Slaughterhouse into his eponymous city. He feared it would cost him money. Hammond had been resorting to elaborate trickery to keep his business costs down. "He wanted the railroads to garner the impression that the plant was not locating permanently here—erected flimsy buildings in order to trick the Michigan Central Railroad officials into believing they could remove themselves with little trouble," according to the *Hammond, Indiana American Bicentennial Yearbook*. "This kept the railroad rates lower and when the Erie & Monon rails were laid he continued to scheme. 'This will never be a permanent location,' he drummed into the railroad officials' minds at every opportunity. The Michigan Central officials were especially worried because for two decades the Hammond packinghouse was one of their top sources of revenue." Beyond the unsettled appearance of shoddy and shabby impermanence, women also were reluctant to settle in Hammond in those fledgling early days because of the heaping piles of bones, cow skulls and horns with rotting flecks of flesh that gave off a noxious, nauseating odor. The few hardscrabble men who inhabited the boardinghouse reportedly amused themselves in the absence of civilization with dogfights and fistfights.

Disaster struck at the turn of the century. A huge fire consumed the G.H. Hammond Meat Company in October 1901, causing $500,000 in damage and putting the company completely out of business less than two years later. "The flimsy frame buildings lasted only a few hours in spite of the equipment rushed on flat cars from Chicago and Michigan City—the time lag was too long," according to the *Hammond, Indiana American Bicentennial Yearbook*. "No lives were lost but 4,500 previously slaughtered pigs were barbecued to a crisp in the holocaust." Firefighters from Hammond, South Chicago, Michigan City and other surrounding towns went to battle the blaze, but they were too late. Immense brick cooler and storage buildings that were purportedly supposed to be fireproof got destroyed as the blazed engulfed the entire plant. "It was almost like daylight at 10 p.m. that evening," Gordon D. Whitney wrote in the *Hammond Historical Society's History of the Hammond Fire Department*. "The wind veered to the north and the sky was filled with debris. The air became so hot and intense that the beef luggers found it almost impossible to breathe." Firemen worked themselves to exhaustion amid a ghastly scene. "The walls from the cattle that were trapped could be heard above the roar of the fire," Whitney added. "But worst of all was the terrible stench that engulfed the whole. The Calumet River was almost covered by fire caused by the burning animal fats and made drafting water out of the river for firefighting impossible. Despite a herculean effort by the fire department and packing house employees aided by many people of Hammond, the packing house was lost."

More than $3 million in investment got burned up, including 3,332 beef carcasses valued at $50 each in the old beef chill room. Firefighters stayed at the scene for two days, but all that was left in the end was "charred and smoking ruins." "Hammond and its people soon found they had suffered an even greater loss," Whitney wrote. "The giant firm announced it would

The W.B. Conkey Plant was on strike when the G.H. Hammond Meat Company packinghouse burned down, putting the fledgling city in an economic bind. *Hammond Public Library.*

not rebuild or even relocate in Hammond and 1,800 men would be out of work. To make matters worse, the new Conkey plant was on a long strike. The double-barreled blast of these events brought this young city to her knees. Slowly and determinedly, however, Hammond began its climb back up the ladder." All that remained was the office that later became home to the Hammond Athletic Club that brought a professional football team to the city.

The blaze would shape the city for years to come. "According to Richard Lytle, vice president of the Hammond Historical Society, the fire burned for three days and even set the nearby river ablaze," Ed Biershenk wrote in *The Times of Northwest Indiana*. "In response, Mayor Armanis F. Knotts, mayor between 1902 and 1904, organized the Hammond Industrial Committee that attracted 11 factories to the city."

Blazes also later destroyed Hammond's carriage factory, the distillery and the Hammond Lumber Company. Another major fire that shaped the city's early history was the Great Hammond Fire, Hammond's own equivalent of the infamous Great Chicago Fire. Chicago might have ended up just another cow town in the Midwest instead of the third-largest city in the United States if Mrs. O'Leary's mythical cow hadn't kicked over a lantern and sparked an epic conflagration that cleared the way for the Loop to be rebuilt with skyscrapers. Such conflagrations were rampant in a time of rapid growth, lumber-framed buildings and lax construction standards. Hammond's blaze raked across the town on Christmas Day 1883. In the absence of any firefighters, the fire consumed the Commercial Block, including a meat cooler, the *Hammond Tribune* newsroom and a carriage factory. "It sometimes appears that the history of a city can be traced through its fires," according to *The Hammond, Indiana American Bicentennial Yearbook*. "The first ones are usually the most devastating since early construction does not assure the safeguards that prevent such fires, and codes will later demand." Much of Hammond was laid to ashes within two hours, but it would soon be rebuilt bigger and better than before. The fledgling but resilient city established a volunteer fire department so it would be better prepared in the future.

2
ICE HARVEST AT WOLF LAKE

A popular destination for windsurfing, fishing and kayaking, Wolf Lake spans across Hammond and neighboring Chicago. The shallow glacially formed lake, almost a puddle on the periphery of the marshland that surrounds Lake Michigan's South Shore, has long triggered jokes from locals, such as that it's home to three-eyed fish or mutant frogs. The gently rippling 804-acre lake partly in Hammond's Robertsdale neighborhood was once supposed to become Wolf Lake State Park. For years, legislators planned to turn Wolf Lake into Indiana's first state park, but the proposal never came to fruition, undone at the last minute because of a little-known statute that prevented state parks from being located inside cities. So the lake was instead turned over to the city to be run as a municipal park on the Indiana side. It's a state park on the Illinois side.

In the early days, Wolf Lake was home to many fishermen, hunters and trappers. They harvested fish, ducks, geese and muskrats that were sold to people in town. For instance, "Charley the Fisherman" kept a shack on the lake and sold local housewives "a mess of fish" for fifteen cents. The lake supplied ice to the Region and beyond during a time when iceboxes were still used for refrigeration. "Wolf Lake proved to be a valuable asset to the area when the Knickerbocker Ice Company started harvesting ice every winter," historian Kenneth J. Schoon wrote in *Calumet Beginnings*. "The 1911 superintendent, Phil Smidt, later established a restaurant nearby." The ice company didn't last long, but Smidt's restaurant lasted nearly a century, serving hundreds of millions of pieces of buttered lake perch under five different owners.

Ice cutters harvested ice from Wolf Lake in the days before refrigeration. *Hammond Public Library.*

Hunting, fishing and trapping at Wolf Lake gave way to commercial ice harvesting operations in the winter. *Hammond Public Library.*

The Knickerbocker Ice Company wasn't the only game in town. The G.H. Hammond Company had as many as two hundred men cutting and storing ice in the era before artificial refrigeration. "The largest single deposit of ice put up in storage during the last week of February 1914 was some 65,000 cubic feet at the Swift and Company Ice Houses located at Wolf Lake," the Hammond Historical Society noted in its *Flashback* newsletter. "It was estimated that this amount of ice would be the equivalent of 5,074,400,000 ice cubes. Thus the harvest from Wolf Lake would be enough to supply ice for fifty-six drinks a year for every person living in the United States at the time." That year was a bonanza for ice companies on Wolf Lake. "Some one half million tons of ice were cut and stores at each of the four Consumer Company ice houses located at Wolf Lake," reported the *Flashback* newsletter. "On average, 22,772.5 tons are stacked in each of the buildings."

During the Cold War, Wolf Lake was home to a Nike missile silo meant to defend both Chicago and the heavy industry in Northwest Indiana. Tragically, many bodies also turned up there over the years. While some were drowning victims, Wolf Lake's isolation made it a popular dumping ground for bodies by Chicago gangsters, serial killers and the notorious thrill

The Knickerbocker Ice Company and other enterprises harvested ice from Wolf Lake. *Hammond Public Library.*

killers Leopold and Loeb. "In the early 1920s, Wolf Lake was dubbed a 'gangland graveyard' by the newspapers and by the police, who frequently found the bodies of gangsters dumped there," Troy Taylor wrote in *Blood, Guns & Valentines*. That history is now largely lost but it's vast and sordid.

The mobster Al Capone disposed of the bodies of Chicago Outfit hitmen John Scalise and Albert Anselmi and rival mob boss Joseph "Hop Toad" Giunta at Wolf Lake. After finding them to be disloyal, he threw a banquet in their honor at a roadhouse called The Plantation in Hammond. There Capone put on a bloody show that would make a lasting impression on all who witnessed it. Troy Taylor recounted the scene in *Blood, Guns & Valentines*:

> *As he addressed his guests—playfully holding a baseball bat to illustrate his lecture on team spirit—he suddenly turned on Scalise, Anselmi and Giunta. "This is how we deal with traitors," he growled and before the men could move, Capone soldiers bound them into their chairs. Capone beat each of the men to within an inch of their lives with the baseball bat. But he didn't kill them. As he stepped away, gunmen approached with their weapons drawn and began firing. Scalise threw up a hand to cover his face and a bullet severed his little finger and slammed into his eye. Another bullet crashed into his jaw and he fell out of his chair. Anselmi's right arm was broken by a bullet. Giunta's chest opened up with the force of the slugs, showering the table in front of him with blood. When the men fell out of their chairs and onto the floor, their assailants stood over them and fired more bullets into their backs.*

The bodies of Guinta, Anselmi and Scalise—who was considered one of the most dangerous and feared hitmen in Prohibition-era Chicago—later turned up at Wolf Lake.

Two of the eight known victims of the Southeast Side serial killer Andrew Urdiales—who prosecutors described as a "savage, predatory, cunning killer"—also were found at Wolf Lake. Urdiales, a former U.S. Marine who suffered from schizophrenic delusions, killed women in Indiana, Illinois and California during the 1990s before he was caught with the help of Hammond Police Department officer Warren Fryer, who had arrested him with a prostitute and an unregistered snub-nosed revolver outside a known crack house and then later identified him as a potential suspect in the serial killings while interviewing street walkers strolling along State Line Road on the border of Hammond and Calumet City. Urdiales was sentenced to death in California in 2018 and killed himself in prison.

Two of the most infamous thrill killers in the history of twentieth-century America also got rid of a body at the notorious dumping grounds. Richard Loeb and Nathan Leopold, rich and intelligent Hyde Park residents, disposed of Bobby Franks's body at Wolf Lake in 1924 in what they tried to make look like a botched kidnapping. "Leopold, who was the oldest of the two at 19, was the first to become fascinated with the idea proposed by Friedrich Nietzsche and his philosophical concept of superior men with capabilities so far above average that they would be exempt from ordinary laws of society. He convinced his 18-year-old friend Loeb to test the immunity-of-superiority theory and the two embarked on a series of crimes including property theft, vandalism and arson," Pat Colander wrote in *The Times*. "The fact that they were not caught for these relatively petty crimes reinforced the idea that they were superior, but it also left them disappointed. When they did not get enough attention or media coverage for their misdeeds, Leopold and Loeb perversely concocted a plan to commit 'the perfect crime,' and murder Bobby Franks, a 14-year-old son of a watch manufacturer who lived in the neighborhood and attended the Harvard School for Boys in the Kenwood area, the same school Loeb had attended."

The icehouses at Wolf Lake produced millions of tons of ice. *Hammond Public Library.*

Icehouses on Wolf Lake at one point stored the equivalent of more than five billion ice cubes. *Hammond Public Library.*

They decided to dump the body in a railroad culvert at Wolf Lake, which Leopold was familiar with because he often went birdwatching there. After nightfall, they poured hydrochloric acid on Franks's face and genitals in the hope of making him harder to identify, but authorities recovered and identified the body in days. The famous attorney Clarence Darrow defended them in what was billed as "the trial of the century," delivering a twelve-hour closing argument that spared them the death penalty. Loeb was murdered in prison, but Leopold was eventually released after publishing an autobiography and lived out the remainder of his days in Puerto Rico.

Wolf Lake's past as a gangland graveyard is largely lost to the passage of time. Today, the 804-acre lake is a pretty placid place, a playground for birdwatchers, fisherman or kayakers. On the Illinois side, it is a state park. West of the Indiana Toll Road that bisects Wolf Lake, it's known as the William W. Powers State Recreation Area. It's estimated more than half a million people visit each year, mainly picnickers and fisherman in search of large-mouth bass, catfish, bluegill, yellow perch, walleye, crappie, northern pike and the other fish there. On the Indiana side, Hammond built a boardwalk and an amphitheater, which it uses to host free bands at Festival of the Lakes and concert acts as diverse as Flo Rida, Nelly, Charlie Daniels and the Steve Miller Band. Today, one is more likely to find a Connecticut warbler there than a bloated water-logged body.

3
ROBY

Snuggled up on the Chicago border, Hammond has long drawn vice-seekers from neighboring Illinois. Smokes are less heavily taxed in Indiana, and recreational fireworks are completely banned in Illinois. Lady Luck also beckons with a flashing marquee that can be seen for miles around. The Horseshoe Casino is a major draw that advertises on billboards across Chicago, sponsors concerts in Millennium Park and runs complimentary shuttles in from Chicago. One of the earlier efforts to lure Chicagoans across the state line occurred in the 1890s when Chicago decided to crack down on poolrooms and racing. The Roby Horse Track opened just across the state line, offering both dog racing and pool just a few feet from the state line in what was billed as "Atlantic City on the Lake." Jacob Forsyth, who originally owned most of the Whiting-Robertsdale area, sold six hundred acres of land north of Wolf River by the Illinois state line to Edward Roby in 1873. It was an idyllic area with wildflowers amid the prairie grass where John Shedd of Shedd Aquarium fame owned most of the rental properties, charging just seven dollars a month to live in such a pastoral setting. The post office there was billed as "the smallest in the world."

Roby eventually partnered with a gambling syndicate from Cicero known as the Columbia Athletic Club, which planned a "grand resort with casinos, hotels and summer homes." Gambling, boxing and racing soon followed. "By 1893 with the coming of thousands to the World's Columbian Exposition on Chicago's South Side, Chicago authorities had come down hard on prostitution and gambling in their midst," *The Times of Northwest*

Left: The Roby Speedway in Hammond drew visitors from far and wide. *Hammond Public Library.*

Below: Boxing was once a popular sport for the gamblers at Roby. *Hammond Public Library.*

Indiana archivist Pat Kincaid wrote. "So 'the boys brought it all to Roby. And while they had talked of grandiose plans for the resort, they found it just as simple to put up a wooden barn and build a horse racing track. And because Chicago disallowed prize fighting, Roby built an arena and held the violent matches there instead." The site sprawled for more than six hundred acres and was heavily wooded. "Prize fighting was also forbidden in Indiana, but the state did permit exhibitions of the 'manly art of self-defense,'" Powell A. Moore wrote in *The Calumet Region: Indiana's Last Frontier.* "Roby was an ideal site for gambling activities. It was believed that the wilderness then separating Roby from Hammond proper would discourage any interference with illegal activities. The place was close to Chicago and only a few miles from the site of the World's Fair which was expected to attract large crowds from all parts of the nation."

Roby was a grand, ambitious operation. "The boxing arena was designed to host 12,000 spectators," Schoon wrote. "At first there was only one racecourse, the Forsythe Track, the back stretch of which was only three miles from the Illinois state line. Two additional tracks, the Lakeside and the Sheffield, were constructed in 1895 following enactment of Indiana law permitting only 15 days of continuous racing at any track and requiring an interval of thirty days between meetings at the same course. By holding meetings of fifteen days at Forsythe, then at Lakeshore and next at Sheffield the gamblers expected to conduct legal racing for several months each year. The syndicate controlled the gambling by permitting only its own bookmakers to operate at the trucks." Though a "primitive" affair with horse tracks that consisted of little more than grandstands around the dirt track, Roby proved to be a huge draw. "Chicagoans and Hoosiers flocked to this sporting center in great numbers, crowds of 6,000 people being common at prizefighters," Schoon wrote. The audience was a little seedy, according to the *Whiting Sun*: "It's the same old crowd that used to visit upper Clark Street, sullen, loud, noisy, and glum at the law which drove them into the wilderness and across the prairie to carry on this tradition."

At first, government officials looked the other way. "Here it was intended to race all the year around by a system of subordination, which gave employment to many persons in the vicinity of the track at extraordinary wages," Ball wrote in *Northwestern Indiana from 1800 to 1900*. "The enmity of the Lake County officials was met and conquered and for three years the Roby track enjoyed immunity from local interference. At the Indiana track the foreign bookmaking, which was really a pool room, was the profitable part of the business." Chicagoans poured in by train and trolley, but Roby's popularity drew unwanted attention. Complaints mounted as the track developed a sleazy reputation. And local governments were not getting a piece of the action. "The gambling at Roby was quite illegal and no tax monies were paid to support local community, so eventually it was shut down," noted Schoon. "In later years Roby was the site of dance halls, amusement parks and restaurants."

Provoked by the boldness of how the syndicate openly advertised its illicit attractions, Indiana governor Claude Matthews eventually waged war on the Roby Horse Track, sending in state militias on raids in 1893 to cancel its Labor Day boxing program. The boxing arena burned down. "But gambling was resumed after troops departed," Moore wrote. "On Sundays, an estimated 1,500 eager customers fought with one another to get to the gambling tables at the casino. Special trains were run from Chicago and the streetcars were frequently so crowded that the tricks to and from the city were made without stopping to pick up passengers along the way." Merchants in Whiting and Hammond and several newspapers began to crusade against the gambling operations. Businesses feared they were losing out on money after finding that slaughterhouse workers were pooling money and sending it to Roby to bet on the races. But Roby reportedly controlled most of the newspapers in Hammond, the city administration and the Lake County sheriff, paying them off to look the other way, according to Moore's *The Calumet Region*. The newspapers of the day accused them of being "Robyized" or entangled in the "Roby Octopus."

The Indiana Supreme Court was outside the sphere of influence and ruled the three tracks were under the same ownership and fell under the restriction that required an interim of thirty days between fifteen-day racing periods, a decision that forced them to reduce races to just the Lakeside Track. Even worse, Chicago tracks reopened seasonally and were far more accessible to the public, drawing business away. The house does in fact sometimes lose. The gambling moguls eventually ran out of luck, Moore opined:

> *In 1905 the era of large-scale gambling came to an end at Roby. In that year the Indiana General Assembly forbade betting on horse races, thereby crippling the sport in the state. At the same time Governor J. Frank Hanley, around by the vice conditions in Hammond, dismissed the city's police commissioners and appointed a new board to enforce the laws. The new officials acted with such vigor that gamblers and other purveyors of vice were driven westward into Illinois. Also, the advance of population and industry into that part of the Region made Roby a less congenial place for illegal activities.*

Hammond later cleaned up the site, which was redeveloped into a shopping mall anchored by a Super Walmart. Like the Roby Track before it, it feeds mainly on business from across the state line.

ROBY SPEEDWAY

At the Chicago border, the little town of Roby, long since swallowed into Hammond, remained a hub for racing even after the state crackdown. After horse racing was driven out, the tracks were repurposed for horse training and then as a motorcycle racing arena because of the popularity of motorcycle shops in the area. As automobiles took off into the 1920s, the Roby Speedway started featuring automotive racing on a one-mile oval dirt track. Sunday tickets cost just $1.10 at the speedway between 108th Street and 122th Street west of Indianapolis Boulevard, about one hundred feet from the Illinois state line. Promoters lured people from both Indiana and Illinois into seats by raffling off 1920 Fords and $500.00 in cash. There was a swamp in the middle of the one-mile dirt track and that was just one of the dangers in a more reckless time—just after World War I—when drivers wore hoods for "mystery races" and even raced an airplane at one point. "Drivers didn't wear helmets and the cars had no roofs," Jerry Murawski told *The Times*. "There were many fatalities as these guys were going 98 mph." The Roby Speedway was the premier auto racing track in Northwest Indiana and for the South Side of Chicago between 1920 and 1936. At each race, thousands of eager fans—some of whom snuck in—packed the wooden stands. "I lived near the track on Fifth Street in what was then Roby," John Mindas told *The Times of Northwest Indiana* in 2011. "We couldn't have been teenagers yet, so during the week we would go up to the back fence, loosen a couple of boards and then come back on Sunday and sneak in."

The speedway drew fans and drivers from across the Calumet Region, greater Chicagoland and the rest of the country, including Detroit, California and Washington State. Drivers included racing legend Duke Nalon, Indianapolis 500 winner Billy Arnold, eventual three-time Indianapolis 500 champion and milk drinker Wilbur Shaw and the murderous bank robber Lester Gillis, better known as Baby Face Nelson. They raced for as many as 75, 100 or 250 miles as fans cheered them on. At the time, it was one of the few racetracks where African American drivers could compete. Many racers who cut their teeth at the Roby Speedway went on to race in the

Indianapolis 500, including Cliff Woodbury and Al Cotey. Jean Shepherd fondly remembered the track surrounded by a wooden fence on his WOR radio show in New York City: "It was right next to the main road that went into Chicago. It was a city street. It would be like if the track were right next to the Merritt Parkway. You would be driving along there on a Sunday going to your grandmother's house of something and you would see this cloud of dust coming out from the racetrack." Shepherd recalled how the races took place every Sunday—leading to long lines of Hudsons backed up on the street—and vendors tried to capitalize by selling ice cream. He recounted the tale of how a race driver crashed through the fence and onto a Grand Pace outside: "There was a hole you could have driven a Mack truck through in that fence. You could see the cars continuing to go past inside." The race driver got out and took the swearing driver in to see the manager. Police hadn't seen a wreck like it before and weren't sure how to handle the situation, such as if the race car driver could be charged with reckless driving. "It made my Old Man's week," Shepherd told listeners. "He was just sorry they didn't get his hup-mobile. He was just sorry he wasn't three to four cars ahead and they didn't get him."

As many as ten thousand fans turned out to see the races there. Spectators dined at the nearby Roby Inn, which was known for having the finest lake perch and frog legs at the time. "Old pictures of the race events showed the grandstands and the infield packed with spectators and such noted drivers as Wilbur Shaw, Rex Mays, Duke Nalon, Ted Horn, Louie Meyer and Babe Stapp challenging the track," *The Times* correspondent Bernie Biernacki wrote. "In the early 1930s black drivers, including Charles Wiggins, raced in their own events at Roby. Death was a constant companion of those early race drivers. A total of six competitors died at Roby. The growing number of driver deaths and an incident when a loose wheel catapulted into the stands severely injuring a number of fans led to the track's demise."

Five spectators were injured on one day in a string of misfortunes. In 1935, a driver suffered burns on his arms and legs when his car caught fire. In 1936, twenty-nine-year-old driver Ray Pixley died at the Roby Speedway after a sixth-place finish at the Indianapolis 500, a great result that convinced the Los Angeles native to remain in the Midwest. He died at Roby three months later while running sixth in the eighth lap of a ten-mile heat race. His car, the Jeter Hisso, struck a tire marker, skidded and flipped. Pixley was flung out of the car, but it then landed on him. The fatalities and lawsuits proved to be too much, according to the *Post-Tribune*. The Roby Speedway was torn apart in 1940, four years after the last race there. Carl Stockholm tried to save it in 1937 but ended up moving all his scheduled races to the Cook County Fairgrounds across the state line in Illinois.

In the twenty-first century, little trace remains of the Roby Speedway, save for the Roby Red Ale at Bulldog Brewing on 119th Street in neighboring Whiting, the poster for which depicts a vintage, open-wheel race car. "Your taste buds will race with excitement as your palate enjoys the caramel malts and English hops that give this robust ale its robust flavor," advertises the craft brewery. "Named for the historic Roby Speedway, tucked between 108th and 112th streets from 1930 to 1936. Pouring its deep red hue, lift a glass to the local daredevils that push the limits just like a good craft brew."

4
WEST HAMMOND

Calumet City, Illinois, on the other side of State Line Road from Hammond, was originally known as West Hammond. The city in Cook County, about nineteen miles south of downtown Chicago, was founded by German Lutheran farmers in 1893. Originally, the settlement was a Hammond suburb, as it was "free of industrial gases and therefore highly desirable for residential purposes," according to the chamber of commerce in 1954. The *Encyclopedia of Chicago* noted, "The early community depended heavily on the factories and commerce of Hammond." West Hammond became a notorious den of vice, filled with speakeasies and gambling parlors, with neon and glitter. As recently as the 1980s, "Sin City" was home to a procession of strip clubs, seedy bars and nightclubs like the Zig Zag Tavern, where women danced on the bars. A sign posted on one storefront claimed that "you must be 21 to enter and have three IDs to prove it." The *Encyclopedia of Chicago* entry continued:

> *When Indiana went dry in 1916, West Hammond became an attractive watering hole for the drinkers of Northwest Indiana. Bootleggers like Al Capone built on this base when national Prohibition came into play, and the town of West Hammond, just 30 minutes from downtown Chicago, gained a reputation as a "Sin City," where gambling, prostitution and illegal booze joints created a pre-Las Vegas strip of State Street. Hardworking residents were so dismayed by the town's bad reputation that they voted in 1923 to change the name to Calumet City.*

Lost Hammond, Indiana

A home in West Hammond, Illinois, which is now Calumet City. *Hammond Public Library.*

Once a haunt for Capone and other mobsters, State Street was lined with garish signs for businesses such as Whiskey-A-Go-Go, which promised, "Beautiful Go Go Girls Nightly." The dancers there were known for wearing festive Santa hats during the holiday season. Home to more than one hundred bars, it was two blocks of show clubs like the Rendezvous and Girl Revue, "burlesque direct from Acapulco," with gaudy signs touting Old Style, Stroh's and Berghoff beers or "Hurricane Donna The Latin American Bombshell" and "Venus and her Jungle Beasts." Men could leer at scantily clad dancers at places like the Sugar Shack and Chesterfield Lounge, according to *The Times of Northwest Indiana* archives.

John Bacino, former owner of John's Pizzeria, reminisced to *The Times*:

> *Back when in its heyday, there were so many people that the sidewalks were full and they had to walk in the street. Back in our heyday, we had damask tablecloths if you can believe it and were more of a dinner restaurant than a pizza place. It's a place where we were in vogue. People would come in and go table-hopping because all their friends were here. It was that type of place and we had that for about 25 years. A lot of good memories, a lot of good people. That's what we miss—the friends we made.*

Calumet City bore nicknames like "Syndicate City" and "Last Chance Gulch." The Chicago Crime Commission went so far as to label it as "the rootin'est, tootin'est, most wide open burg this side of the Butte" and "probably the greatest concentration of low-brow whoopee in the western hemisphere and well able to give Place Pigalle in Paris a run for its money."

Various civic groups and mayors waged war against the State Street bars, honkytonks and vice dens for most of the twentieth century. Virginia Brooks took matters into her own hands, and Kym Liebler wrote of her efforts in *The Times*:

> *An outraged Brooks assembled a feisty group of women called the "Brooks Black Brigade" to crack down on the unsavory acts on State Street and State Line Road in what was then called West Hammond. They raided brothels and, according to city folklore, literally ripped the houses of ill repute apart, using umbrellas and hatpins for weapons. The Brooks Black Brigade, so dubbed because the women wore black hats, shoes and umbrellas, successfully exposed prostitution and the drug dealing on the strip and gained attention throughout the Midwest in the process. Brooks left West Hammond in 1913, but the problem remained.*

Calumet Memorial Park in West Hammond, which has since been renamed Calumet City. *Hammond Public Library.*

Mayor Jerry Genova, whose grandfather ran a long-gone hot dog stand in Cal City named Moe's, finally succeeded in the 1990s. "What happened back in 92–93 is we had a lot of prostitution issues, strip clubs and liquor stores, a lot of crime issues," Genova told *The Times*. "I suppose the most poignant time in my life was sitting in my new home. I had a mortgage, I had a new baby on the way, and each morning I would read the newspaper, and I would read about prostitution and deficits and crime and homicides and think, 'what did I get myself into here?' I'm in charge of this. That's when I decided to take an aggressive approach." He got the strip clubs and taverns torn down and personally appealed to nearby residents to relocate, ensuring they got enough money in their settlements to move to new homes. "One of the sadder parts of my tenure is that I had to take down those old neighborhoods," Genova said. "But progress comes."

Hobbled by shifting demographics and declining property values, Calumet City is no longer much of a destination for vice or anything else, save for the trade district that's limping along around the struggling River Oaks Center mall or perhaps to a lesser extent the Cook County Forest Preserves. In 2016, the erstwhile strip along State Street was described as "a sad wasteland" and "a rundown dump with boarded-up stores." "We went through a lot of good times and bad times and moving south times," Bacino told *The Times*.

The neon lights of West Hammond have flickered out and the beer taps run dry, but one vice lives on along State Street on the border of Calumet City and downtown Hammond. The Hammond Police Department often runs prostitution stings in which officers nab johns trying to pick up streetwalkers. And though Calumet City purged the vice trade and street gangs like the Gangster Disciples, Vice Lords, Latin Counts and Four Corner Hustlers that gained footholds in the 1980s and 1990s, the city remains plagued by crime—with more than ten murders in a typical year and substantially more violent crime than the U.S. average, according to city-data.com. "Although the apartment complex area and northeast side are much better than before, these areas still remain the roughest areas in the village and experience the highest crime," comments the Chicago Gang History website. "The village also still pulls in high rates of crime and is one of the more troubled suburbs in Chicagoland."

5
FIVE POINTS

Not far from the Chicago border and the Lake Michigan shoreline, the intersection of Indianapolis Boulevard, Calumet Avenue and East 114th Street on Hammond's far north side, a crossroads with five spokes, has long been a hub of activity in the city, a focal point for dining, entertainment and industry. "The main intersection in town was, of course, at State and Hohman, the Four Corners. However, Five Points at the junction of Indianapolis and Calumet had a fame of its own," O'Hern wrote in the Hammond Historical Society's *Pages from the Past.* "Besides being an important place to make streetcar transfers, Five Points was also famous for its amusement park, with roller coaster and all, on the site of Lever Brothers. Also, at or near the Five Points were several dance halls, Phil Smidt's and Levent's restaurants and the Roby Race Track." It was a dining destination in the early twentieth century. "At Five Points, the intersection of Indianapolis Boulevard, Calumet Avenue, and 114th Street, several wonderful restaurants served specialties like lake perch and frog legs," Kimberly Eck and Jennifer Linko wrote in *Whiting and Robertsdale.* "Phil Smidt's was the longest lasting restaurant, serving the area for 97 years before closing in 2007. In 1939, for $1.25, patrons could feast on all-you-can-eat perch, swimming in butter." Phil Smidt's outlasted another popular restaurant at Five Points, Margaret's Geneva House. "Margaret Winkelried Carroll, the proprietor, did much of the cooking herself," Eck and Linko noted. "Her parents opened the Geneva House in 1913, bringing new touches not yet seen in other local fish houses, such as a real floor, white tablecloths, and European-style service. Much of Margaret's business came from Chicago."

Five Points was once the center of the universe in Hammond. *Hammond Public Library.*

ATHEY HYDRO AMUSEMENT PARK

The Athey Hydro Amusement Park opened on one thousand acres of land by Wolf Lake and Indianapolis Boulevard in 1914. It offered aeroplanes, flying boats, music, boating, a hot air balloon, a merry-go-round, a German beer garden with a cabaret and a thirty-foot promenade with a number of concessions. The Hammond Historical Society said of the amusement park in its *Flashback* newsletter:

> *Jinxed from the beginning, upon its opening the Athey Hydro Park was doomed from the very start. Many of the shows and attractions at the park were not up and running. Those who attended the grand opening of the park were nearly eaten alive or carried away by the large swarms of mosquitoes who made the tall thickets of grass their home. To remedy this problem park building and operator I.H. Athney purchased a dozen barrels of oil from the nearby Standard Oil Co. and saturated the water with it.*

Hammond is a little more environmentally conscious now and even operates the Hammond Environmental Center on Calumet Avenue by Lake George. But even after vanquishing the mosquitoes through less than aboveboard means, the amusement park didn't last long. Within a few months, a smoldering cigar butt ignited the German beer tent and burned the whole place down. "The fire spread so rapidly the tent burned in less than 10 minutes," *Flashback* reported. "The arch was blown down to the ground and demolished with the part of the large fence that surrounds the park. Many of the promised aerial exhibitions and stunts never materialized, because something would always happen to stop the flights." Then two different storms with gale-force winds destroyed the planes and the rest of the park, forcing its ultimate shutdown.

MADURA'S DANCELAND

For decades, Madura's Danceland at Five Points in Hammond was one of the most happening spots in the Region. It was exciting. "The streetcar would pull up to Five Points in Hammond, the conductors would yell 'danceland!' and everyone would disembark for an evening of twirling across the velvety wooden floor known throughout Northwest Indiana and Chicago," *The Times of Northwest Indiana* community editor Sharon Rocchio wrote. As Region historian and *The Times* columnist Archibald McKinlay put it, "Its springy floors served generations of itchy feet." Mike Madura II and Mickey Madura ran Madura's Danceland for forty years until it was struck by lightning in July 1967 and burned down while the owners were in church. It hosted many trendy dance marathons and big-band orchestras, bringing together countless Region couples. "It was a family business and we were all involved in it," Marcia Madura Kozlowski told *The Times*. "I started working there in the coat check room when I was 13." Mike Madura bought the dance hall building in 1929 and moved it across the street with a wagon and a team of horses. The lights and toilets were broken in the process, but the dance floor remained intact. Kozlowski remembered Danceland fondly in a 2003 *Times* article when the places became one of the few defunct businesses to be commemorated with a South Shore Line poster. "The floor was wonderful—my dad and grandfather had special waxes they mixed together for just the right finish," she told *The Times*. "You wanted it shiny but at the same time it couldn't be so slick that people would fall."

Madura's Danceland was indeed the centerpiece of Five Points and a sight to behold. "Even today when you talk to people who went to Madura's Danceland, one of the first things they speak of was its beautiful and highly polished dance floor," Whiting-Robertsdale Chamber of Commerce executive director Gayle Faulkner Kosalko wrote in a letter to *The Times* in 2002. Kosalko recalled, "Every night Mike and his son, Mike Jr., had a ritual for cleaning the floor. They made their own special floor cleaner by grinding dance wax and paraffin together in a huge meat grinder. Dance wax alone would leave the floor too slippery for the 2,000 customers each night." The dancehall was featured in Lou Galt's book *Ballroom Echoes*. It also lived on vividly in many memories. "But much of the history of the romantic place is written down in local church wedding registries because an incredible amount of couples met there for the very first time," Kosalko commented. "My in-laws are one of the many couples who met at Madura's. Of the four evenings that Madura's was opened each week, Sunday was truly for romantic couples. This was waltz night, and the mood was set with beautiful colored lights that switched from hue to hue."

Madura's Danceland had a domed roof and marquee lights. As many as three thousand people danced the night away to a full orchestra helmed by a tuxedoed bandleader. People dressed to impress. "Women wore long, flowy dresses and men decked out in the required shirts and ties for dances held at least four nights a week, with waltzes the specialty on Sundays," Rocchio wrote in *The Times*. "People whirled around the floor doing fox trots, swing, rumba and other numbers in those days when couples really knew how to dance and dance together." Both the shimmy and liquor were banned. Ladies paid thirty cents and gents paid forty cents to see orchestra leaders like Jimmy Dorsey, Vaughn Monroe, Guy Lombardo, Ray Anthony, Paul Whiteman and Gene Krupa, who were advertised with window displays. "It was a wonderful time and so romantic," Kozlowski told *The Times*. "I've had many people tell me that was the place they either met or went there with their future spouse."

Big band eventually fell out of favor, but Madura's Danceland adapted to the changing times by becoming a venue for parties, proms and teen dances. "The business never closed its doors, but we did have to change," Kozlowski added. "There's nothing like it anymore. The [South Shore Line] poster is a tribute to all the people of the Calumet Region and Chicago who met there and danced there."

It was the kind of magical place that generated a lot of nostalgia and was where people could forget their daily struggles. "Madura's Danceland in

North Hammond at Five Points packed them in every weekend and holidays and accommodated all ages from 18 to 89," wrote Schererville resident Pat Tuleja in a letter to *The Times of Northwest Indiana* in 2008. "No one did it better than Madura's. Prom night at Madura's in the 1950s was the dream of every senior couple who loved to dance."

INDIANA GARDENS SKATING RINK

Five Points also was home to the popular Indiana Gardens Skating Rink, the predecessor to Madura's Danceland, where kids skated to live organ music before it burned down due to insufficient pressure from local fire hoses. "Today when you drive by Five Points in Robertsdale you see the Purple Steer Restaurant, a liquor store, an Amoco station and Lever Brothers," Kosalko wrote in a letter to *The Times*. "It's hard to believe that this was once the hot spot in the area for entertainment, but it was."

BOARDWALK PARK

Boardwalk Park opened at Five Points in Hammond in 1926. It was so resplendent it was often confused with the White City amusement park on 63rd Street on the South Side of Chicago. The amusement park featured what Shields described as "an awe-inspiring carnival of attractions" that included a 60-foot-tall Ferris wheel, the Whip, a water chute, a miniature railroad, a merry-go-round, a shooting gallery and the King Bee Coaster, which was billed as the biggest roller coaster in the Midwest at the time. *The Times of Northwest Indiana* columnist Larry Shields wrote that "the huge, steep roller coaster ride that encircled the perimeter of the grounds… plunged 90-feet to take away your breath and your bucks." The King Bee was built by Mal Tallion, a carpenter for more than sixty years who built more than a dozen 130-foot coasters in Ohio's Coney Island, Buenos Aires, Venezuela and the 1939 World's Fair. His roller coaster in Hammond was described as "death-defying," but the amusement park lasted for only three years, from 1926 to 1929.

"When I was a lad, my parents took me on weekends to an amusement park at Five Points in Robertsdale," Harold Tratebas wrote in *The Times*.

"It was famed for its huge, steep roller coaster ride that encircled the perimeter of the grounds. The Depression years took their toll of it; the defunct park was razed to make room for construction of a new Lever Bros. plant about 1934." Despite its "monster" roller coaster that drew in thrill seekers, Boardwalk Park ultimately was a relic of another era, Shields noted. "Not that playlands have gone the way of dinosaurs," he wrote. "The Walt Disney theme parks and the Six Flags chain have spread across the nation, operating year around where the weather is hospitable and where there are affluent grandparents." The area also was home to the Hammond Beach Inn nightclub—where the Hammond Marina lies now—and a zoo between Calumet Avenue and Lake Avenue in Robertsdale. "The location for all this entertainment was ideal because folks could step off the streetcar and be right there within a short walking distance," Kosalko added.

HAMMOND BEACH INN

The Hammond Beach Inn is another bygone Five Points attraction. Located where the Hammond Marina is now, the Hammond Beach Inn was "colossal" and aspired to be "the most popular summer lake resort in the Middle West," Region historian Archibald McKinlay wrote in his *Times* column. The two-hundred-by-one-hundred-foot Hammond Beach Inn attracted overflow crowds for the whole weekend when it opened in the summer of 1915.

It was quite a sight to behold.

"The building was handsomely outfitted and enhanced by decorations that adorned the walls," McKinlay wrote. "Thousands of panes of glass windows, suggesting a colonial style to some and a French style to others, could be opened to transform the resort into an open-air building. On the Lake Michigan side, a spacious veranda, 20 feet wide, extended to within a few feet of Lake Michigan." People flocked from all over to eat, dance, swim, fish, boat and enjoy high-class entertainment. Ads promised the opportunity to "bathe, dine and dance." People arrived by trolley and car, taking advantage of a sprawling parking lot that could accommodate one thousand vehicles. Street cars ferried people up Indianapolis Boulevard, discharging them en masse at Five Points, where a miniature train took them to the beach.

The defunct *Whiting Call* newspaper reported that "immense crowds kept coming and going until one might be led to believe the entire states of

Illinois and Indiana had turned out by force." A massive 150-foot-by-80-foot dining room served fish and chicken dinners to thousands, with long lines jostling to get in. The live entertainment included opera singers, exhibition dancers and live orchestras, including Professor Branch's famed orchestra. More than 150 couples could take to the dance floor at the same time during the height of a dance craze. McKinlay noted the Hammond Beach Inn was one of "an amazing variety of amusements at Five Points, Wolf Lake and Roby," that included amusement parks, the speedway, a hydroplane, a baseball park and a half-dozen fish houses, some of which served hooch that was banned during Prohibition.

"While it lasted, it was the anchor of an immense amusement complex that peaked in the 1920s and whose main street had no name," McKinlay wrote. One of his readers suggested the nameless street be called the "Boulevard of Broken Dreams." The resort disintegrated over time and eventually became a location for trysts. "There were literally thousands," Mickey Madura wrote in a letter to *The Times*, "enough condoms on both floors of the Hammond Beach Inn to start a tire factory."

EMPRESS CASINO

Just north of Five Points, the Empress Casino opened in Hammond in 1996 as a four-level fifty-four-thousand-square-foot riverboat on Lake Michigan that was a sister to the popular Egyptian-themed Empress Casino in Joliet. It was established by Jack Binion, who is still the namesake of the Zagat-rated steakhouse with lakefront views known for its celebrated filet mignon and creamed spinach. The State of Indiana initially had cruising requirements, so the casino could only allow new customers every few hours when it was "out sailing," even when the boat was docked on the ice-choked lake during the winter, leaving shivering gamblers waiting on the pier in an almost Kafkaesque bureaucratic limbo.

The Empress was closer to the Loop in Chicago than the casinos now known as Ameristar in East Chicago, Majestic Star in Gary and Blue Chip in Michigan City. It proved to be a hit. By 1997, it averaged $16.6 million in revenue a month, significantly more than the Joliet casino that spawned it, according to the *Chicago Tribune*. The Hammond casino was sold to the Horseshoe Gaming Holding Corporation in 1999 and rebranded as the Horseshoe Casino Hammond, a brand under which it still operates today.

Above: The Empress Casino opened in 1996 as a Lake Michigan riverboat. *Hammond Public Library.*

Left: The Empress Casino was docked next to the Hammond Marina. *Hammond Public Library.*

Above: The Concierge Club Suite gave gamblers a place to lounge at the Empress Casino in Hammond. *Hammond Public Library.*

Opposite, left: The bar at the Bluewater Lounge at the Empress Casino in Hammond kept the drinks flowing. *Hammond Public Library.*

Opposite, right: The Empress Casino is now known as the Hammond Horseshoe Casino and is expected to change hands again soon. *Hammond Public Library.*

The days of faux lake cruises, as well as all the ersatz Egyptian pomp, are long gone. The Horseshoe is now the most popular and successful casino in Indiana and greater Chicagoland, though the Illinois state legislature finally decided to grant Chicago a casino of its own in 2019 and a rival Hard Rock Casino was planned off the Borman Expressway in neighboring Gary.

LEVER BROTHERS/UNILEVER SOAP FACTORY

While many of the recreational attractions at Five Points have long since faded, the Unilever Soap factory at 1200 South Calumet Avenue in Hammond has cranked out soap a short distance from the Chicago border for nearly a century. It is, however, no longer the same major employer with the landmark Rinso sign that was central to city life. Nestled amid railroad tracks and heavy industry, the plant long but no longer known as Lever Brothers at the Five Points intersection started in 1930 on the site of a former amusement park next to Lake Michigan, from which it's always drawn water. Over the years, the brick-clad factory made many different brands of bar soap; the All and Rinso detergents; the Spry, Sunlight and Lux dishwashing liquids; the Imperial and Promise margarines; and Mrs. Butterworth syrup. It made the Lifebuoy soap that Ralphie gets his mouth washed out with after swearing in *A Christmas Story*, prompting a fantasy that it blinds him, driving

Lever Brothers has been making soap in Hammond for nearly ninety years. *Hammond Public Library.*

his parents mad with guilt and regret. The factory long snowed soap flakes on homes in the nearby Robertsdale neighborhood. "My family lived in the Robertsdale neighborhood of north Hammond nestled between a popcorn factory, Lever Brothers, and the Amoco refinery," Indiana University Northwest student Andrew Laurinec wrote in *Steel Shavings.* "Depending on the wind direction, you'd either smell popcorn, soap or whatever kind of noxious gas the oil plant was burning off at the time. Sometimes at night Lever Brothers would release a cloud of smoke and God knows what else into the air. It was not unusual to see people washing their cars early in the morning. After all, there was already soap on their car."

A box of Rinso Soap, one of Lever's best-known and signature products, crowned a forty-foot tower rising from the factory at Five Points in the 1940s. It is described on the Hammond High School Class of 1959 website, long run by former Hammond Historical Society president Richard Barnes

> *Whenever our parents would drive north on Calumet Avenue toward Lake Michigan, kids would start searching the Hammond skyline for the box*

of Rinso soap. It was a cherished landmark to every civic minded kid from Hammond. It was right up there with the Leaning Tower of Pisa, the Empire State Building and the pyramids of Egypt! And it was ours! Hammond kids going to Boy Scout Camp or visiting with other kids in Chicago would always brag about our box of Rinso soap "ten stories tall." The height and size of the Rinso Soap box could be embellished depending on how much was necessary to impress the listener.

By all accounts, it was majestic. The *Calumet Region Historical Guide* said the factory represented "the highest type of industrial architecture in the Region."

"One of the largest soap plants in the world, it is considered the most modern," according to the Writers' Project of the Works Progress Administration. "Constructed of tan pressed brick, it would have the appearance of a civic institution were it not for the 40-foot reproduction of a box of Rinso which surmounts the main building." The massive plant included a soapery, glycerine building, bleachery, melting-out building, finishing building, warehouse and tank farms for vegetable shortening. It was once open to public tours. "Tours start in the lobby of the finishing building and proceed to the soapery, where the chief point of interest is the kettle room where fats, oils and soda are boiled down in kettles three stories high and 20 feet in diameter," according to the *Calumet Region Historical Guide*. "The visitors' attention is directed particularly to the spiral coils of steam pipes at the bottom of each kettle and the ventilator over each. The carefully proportioned solutions of oil and caustics bubbling within these kettles represent every stage of the four-day boiling down process which is the first step in soap and glycerine making." Workers in "industrial pajamas" made Rinso, Lifebuoy health soap, Lux flakes, Lux and Pears toilet soap and Spry and Covo vegetable shortening. Work there was difficult, and the hours were long. Maurey Zlotnik wrote in the Hammond Historical Society's *Pages from the Past*:

> After high school, I worked for two years at Lever Brothers. One night in August I talked with this fellow about possibly changing my time of work. I was packing Rinso, $21.60 a week, ten at night until six in the morning except on Sunday from twelve to six. I thought I could possibly change my hours so I could go to DePaul in Chicago. He said, "I don't want any dog-gone college kids working for me." Only he said it in a little stronger terms. So I went home and packed my grip and the next morning I got my pay and hitch-hiked to Terre Haute. I never came home all year.

The Lever Brothers laundry plant soap was expanded and remodeled in 1954. In 1980, a $43 million expansion doubled the plant's capacity to stamp out bars of soap, making it the "most modern bar soap plant in the world."

In 1995, its British owner, the multinational consumer goods giant that produces 150 consumer goods products like Ben & Jerry's ice cream, Skippy peanut butter and Hellmann's mayonnaise, grossing more than $62 billion in revenue in 2017, was rebranded as Unilever. At that point, the factory produced only Dove, Caress, Suave and Lever 2000 bars of soap, according to *The Times of Northwest Indiana*. Employment plunged from 1,600 in the 1970s to a few hundred workers as automation reshaped the manufacturing industry. But Hammond's soap plant remained as productive as ever. In 2005, the factory produced 2.5 million bars of soap per day, making all the Dove soap sold in North America. "In the past 25 years, the company has invested over $180 million in the factory and built two state-of-the-art manufacturing complexes," human resources manager Christopher Cole told *The Times* at the Hammond plant's Diamond Jubilee in 2005. "With an operating budget of over $60 million, improvements here are continual."

The Lever Brothers plant at Five Points is now known as Unilever after it was bought out by the multinational conglomerate. *Hammond Public Library.*

The Lever Brothers factory that once made Rinso detergent was once considered the "most modern soap factory in the world." *Hammond Public Library.*

But the Lever Brothers plant, formerly a central part of the community, is no longer the major landmark it once was, lacking the enormous Rinso sign that once turned heads of passing motorists. Today, it employs a fraction of the people it once did and makes far fewer products. Though Unilever supports charitable causes in the community, many current Hammond residents could not even tell you what is produced there now. "Region residents were initially concerned that the plant would be a 'stink factory,' producing noxious odors over residential areas," *The Times* writer Kathleen Dorsey wrote in the South Shore in 100 Objects series. "But on the contrary, the factory's soap products can still be smelled over the lakeshore today, giving off a fresh scent reminiscent of laundry days gone by."

6
DOWNTOWN

Downtown Hammond once was a major regional hub for shopping and entertainment, the place to go for more than seven decades. Department stores, glitzy cinemas and lunch counters lined Hohman Avenue. According to the *Encyclopedia of Chicago*,

> *Hammond developed an impressive regional downtown with department stores, office blocks, and movie palaces. In addition, the 1920s produced a housing boom. A few of the new subdivisions south of downtown were exclusive, like Woodmar, which promised to move residents "out of the smoke zone and into the ozone" and provided work for local architects L. Cosby Bernard and Addison Berry. But most new homes were modest bungalows.*

In the 1920s, downtown Hammond was home to medicine shows where banjo players or Native Americans drew crowds before a salesman launched into a pitch, claiming some tonic cured his rheumatism or his sciatica or some other condition. "One of the big places for medicine shows was in downtown Hammond about where Rosalee's is now," Maurice O'Hern recalled in the Hammond Historical Society's *Pages from the Past*. "At one time they advertised they were showing the Cardiff Giant. He was supposed to be in back of the stage behind a curtain. I went over and stood around and the man said, 'Go ahead and see it.' So I went it in. Here it was, a stone man. It didn't impress me much. It just looked awful

Modern-day downtown Hammond as viewed from the Hohman Avenue Bridge. *Photo by the author.*

dead. So I just walked out and the man got mad. He said I was supposed to put a nickel or a dime in the can."

In the 1950s, more than 27,500 vehicles passed through downtown Hammond per day, making it one of the most heavily trafficked parts in Lake County, according to the *Calumet District Traffic Survey Report*. With department stores like Goldblatt's and Minas, the city's commercial district drew shoppers from Munster, Highland, East Chicago, Whiting, Lansing, Calumet City and other adjacent communities. Shoppers spent more than $135 million a year at an estimated 1.1 million square feet of retail space in downtown Hammond in the mid-1950s. "Within this trade area other shopping districts also compete for trade, but Hammond is the dominant retail center," the Purdue Calumet Development Foundation wrote in its 1958 report *An Urban Improvement Program for Hammond, Indiana*.

In the 1920s, downtown Hammond was home to the Kuhn's meat market, Tittle's meat market, an A&P store, Seitzer's Grocery, the Hoess Brothers' Machine Shop, the Waltz bicycle shop, the Schulte Cigar Store, Griswold's Hardware store and the Scatena's ice cream emporium. "Scatena's, with

Hohman Avenue in downtown Hammond. *Photo by the author.*

its wire-back chairs and wire-legged tables had a cool and delightful atmosphere that exuded the charms of ice cream soda and sundaes," O'Hern wrote in the Hammond Historical Society's *Pages from the Past*. "It was the same Scatena that sponsored the Hammond football team." Jackie Diamond's was a produce store that was open year-round but open-air in the summer months. Humpfer's Market displayed pike and other fish in iced cases on the sidewalk. Seifer's Furniture Store had a large balloon moored to the top of the building. "It was quite an attention getter," O'Hern wrote. "Certainly, it attracted the attention of 12-year-old boys." He and his friends also frequented the Millikan's and Colonial's Sport Stores, gaping at display windows that O'Hern recalls were filled with "guns, hunting knives, tents, canoes, shells, binoculars, football gear, baseballs, gloves, bats, basketballs, fishing gear and ice skates." Downtown was the place to be. O'Hern described it as the "center of the universe." He wrote:

> *People, streetcars, trucks, wagons—what a maelstrom. On the northeast corner was the Coney Island Restaurant. The area outside this restaurant was chronically jammed with people waiting to catch streetcars. And as*

you waited for the cars on a cold day, the fragrance of broiling frankfurters, with the connotation of warmth and comfort was almost unbearable. On the northwest corner, there was the Walgreens Drug Store. When times were really flush we'd be treated to a 25-cent malted milkshake at Walgreens. The shakes were served with a large dollop of whipped cream. As we put our noses into the glass to enjoy the milkshakes we sometimes came up with a daub of whipping cream on our noses.

Architect George F. Lovall designed the three-story Schneider Department Store at State Street and Morton Court for owner Hyman Schneider for more than $250,000. The full-line department stores sold clothing for all ages from infant to adult, as well as yard goods, luggage and travel products.

With neon and the throngs of people, downtown Hammond really came alive on the weekends. But nothing lasts forever as O'Hern pointed out:

Then there was the grand night of the week downtown—Saturday night, when the stores stayed open. Everyone, so it seemed, went downtown to hop or just to make chance encounters with friends and acquaintances. The

Liberty Hall was built in downtown Hammond in one day in 1918 to help raise money for World War I. *Hammond Public Library.*

Liberty Hall in downtown Hammond served as a recruitment and bond sales office during World War I. The building no longer stood by the mid-1920s. *Hammond Public Library.*

> *wonder of it all. Traffic jams, streetcar jams. Policeman walking beats. Salvation Army units with their devoted groups of musicians and singers playing Gospel music at the Christian preaching. This they would do in all kinds of weather. Preaching, shopping, meeting friends, streetcars, jitneys, autos, trains, stores, charlatans selling gimmicks on street corners, and people, people, people. Gone—all gone.*

Suburbanization killed downtown shopping throughout the country and in neighboring Gary, but downtown Hammond's decline was partly brought on by railroads. "One of Hammond's most long-standing and widely recognized problems is the presence of the many railroads, and their crossings in that heavily trafficked and closely built-up area," according to the *An Urban Improvement Program for Hammond, Indiana* study. Downtown Hammond also suffered from a lack of parking, especially relative to its newly minted suburban rivals. Its 4,042 parking spaces were "inadequate by modern standards" when the *Urban Improvement Program* study came out in the late 1950s. Traffic downtown started to decline in the late 1950s because of the Woodmar Mall at Indianapolis Boulevard and 165th Street in south Hammond and the new Highland Ultra Plaza just south of the city in neighboring Highland. It continued to decline as the population shifted to more suburban pastures farther south and more shopping alternative cropped up like the Southlake and Century malls in Merrillville. "By 1960, Hammond had no room for expansion. However, in 1966, the creation of River Oaks shopping mall in Calumet City challenged Hammond's 70-year history as a center for retailing," noted the Chicago Historical Society's *Encyclopedia of Chicago*. "During the next decade, long-established family businesses closed and a wave of demolition gutted the once-prosperous downtown. Similarly, major industries closed, including American Steel Foundries in 1973, Pullman-Standard in 1981, and Rand McNally in 1981. Only Saint Margaret's Hospital and the First Baptist Church continued to prosper downtown."

Hammond historian Lance Trusty wrote that downtown was hollowed out despite Hammond's population falling by only a few thousand during

The Barelli's appliance and furniture store was the type of retail that used to be in downtown Hammond. *Hammond Public Library.*

the 1980s, a period when the rest of the Region's urban core and Rust Belt cities from across the country declined cataclysmically. Though Hammond was "seemingly the least changed city in the Calumet," the downtown looked like a war zone, Trusty wrote in *Steel Shavings*. "State Street in Hammond resembled a devastated European city of 1945," Trusty commented in the *End of an Era: The 1980s in the Calumet Region* edition of the long-running publication.

Some life remained on Hohman Avenue even after Goldblatt's, the very heart and soul of Old Hammond, closed. But *The Hammond Times* escaped to Munster to become The Times of somewhere, and NIPSCO, after remodeling a major building, moved its engineering and planning divisions to a vacant insurance building in Merrillville. Downtown Hammond's chief tenants were the growing St. Margaret Hospital Complex, the First Baptist Church, NIPSCO's corporate headquarters, banks, and one bustling retailer, the Army & Navy Store. The old downtown had gone the way of the trolley car and the buggy whip. The expenditure of large sums on street improvements along Hohman Avenue had little effect on the decline, and as stores moved out either plywood panels of St. Margaret Hospital moved in Probably both the Gary and Hammond 'downtowns' should be donated to Caterpillar or Komatsu for use as bulldozer testing sites, then returned to nature."

Hammond lost the headquarters of the only Fortune 500 company to be based in Northwest Indiana. Beefed up far beyond most regional utilities by steel mills, oil refineries and other heavy industrial users of electricity in the Region, NIPSCO had been in downtown Hammond before it relocated its operations to its corporate headquarters down in Merrillville. The longest public utility strike in the United States took place in downtown Hammond in 1980, when the utility had about one million customers and five thousand employees. They voted to strike for better wages and benefits, and the strike dragged on for 246 days. "For months before the strike NIPSCO was stockpiling food, bedding and other supplies while maintaining publicly that negotiations were proceeding smoothly," Jeff Sinder wrote in *Steel Shavings*. "With whopping rate increases and controversy over its proposed Bailly nuclear plant, NIPSCO had become the utility that many residents loved to hate."

Striking workers took on other jobs, like mopping up VFW halls, painting houses, cleaning people's garages and hauling junk to the dump. They worked as pipe fitters, security guards and barbers. "Union members also received a little money for picket duty," Sinder wrote. "In December of 1980,

NIPSCO fielded a women's basketball team back when it was still headquartered in downtown Hammond. *Hammond Public Library.*

the union held a Christmas party. Each child received a gift and the parents enjoyed all the goodies. It was a better Christmas party than NIPSCO ever had. Channel Five News from Chicago even showed up to cover it." NIPSCO is now based in a low-slung suburban campus in Merrillville amid the headquarters of other companies like Centier, the largest privately owned bank in Indiana, and MonoSol, which makes dissolvable film for Tide Pods and other single-use detergent packets. NIPSCO parent company the Northern Indiana Public Service Corporation sold three buildings to the Hammond Development Corporation in 2000 and, at the time, still used an office at Hohman Avenue and Russell Street. The corporation was eventually delisted from the Fortune 500 after spinning off its higher-growth pipeline business in 2015, reducing its market capitalization.

Downtown Hammond also lost its streetcar system, which was once the main way to get around. The city is still home to the last interurban in the country, the South Shore Line, which stretches from Chicago to South Bend, ferrying many commuters into the Windy City. But the downtown was once home to electrified streetcars that took people to and fro; they preceded the South Shore Line and its famous "Just Around the Bend" poster series by sixteen years. A streetcar franchise was established along a two-mile stretch of Hohman Avenue downtown in 1892. The Hammond, Whiting and East Chicago Railway Company took over the following year, operating it until 1939. It was backed up by horsepower in case the electricity failed and connected to the Chicago streetcar at the Illinois state line, giving Hammond residents easy access to the Loop. "The streetcar system generally brought more prosperity to Hammond merchants and more people to our city," boasted the *Hammond, Indiana American Bicentennial Yearbook*. "The railroad trains did not cater to the commuters especially, though in 1907 there were 51 trains running daily from Hammond to Chicago and 49 returning here."

O'Hern remembered streetcars as the main form of city transportation in the Hammond Historical Society book *Pages from the Past*. The whole city was then crisscrossed with tracks. "Memories of the streetcar include almost unendurable waits in cold and blowing weather," O'Hern wrote. "But then there was the unbelievable warmth and comfort of the car, with the electric heaters under the seat, when the car finally came. Then there was the high-speed run from Five Points down Sheffield to Hohman. The motorman really opened up along the non-stop part of the route. The car would twist and lurch until it seemed that the ends of the car were going in different directions." As a child, O'Hern was always fascinated by watching the conductor switch trolleys at the end of the station, because the electric-powered cars would give off giant blue sparks when separated by the power line. "Occasionally, as you rode along, the single track would become two tracks," O'Hern added. "The purpose of the second track was to provide a waiting spot for the car until a car coming from the other direction came by. This, of course, allowed the cars to pass each other. To get on the bypass track the motorman had to get off the car and throw the switch manually." Jitneys, an early precursor to Uber and Lyft, were a briefly popular way to get around downtown Hammond in the early 1920s. The few who had cars would supplement their incomes by driving people short distances up and down main street for a nickel. One could only travel straight ahead for a few blocks, but jitneys caught on quickly. Though ultimately a short-lived phenomenon, *jitney* became synonymous with a nickel in Hammond for years to come.

Downtown also was a hub for telephonic communication in the early days. Local businessmen in Hammond persuaded the Chicago Telephone Company to establish the first switchboard in Oscar Krimbill's drugstore on State Street. A telephone exchange building on Rimbach by Goldblatt's went up in 1902, serving one thousand telephones within a few years. It doubled in size in 1913 and then moved to the new Roscoe Woods real estate office in 1925 and then to a newly constructed building on Fayette in 1953. Operators there asked "number, please?" until automatic dialing became prevalent by 1960. At its peak, the operation employed 475 workers who connected seventy thousand telephones in Hammond, East Chicago, Whiting, Highland and Munster.

Downtown Hammond has diminished as a daytime employer and also as a hub of nightlife. One of many short-lived nightclubs to make a splash in Northwest Indiana and then suddenly disappear, AquaVor shuttered in 2013, putting about thirty people out of work. After an initial investment of more than $2 million, the nightclub on the 5200 block of Hohman Avenue said it was forced to close by Hammond's parking lot ordinance that restricted parking in municipal lots between midnight and 5:00 a.m. It had stayed open until 3:00 a.m. Friday and Saturday and lost business when "no parking" signs went up and cars started getting towed. Hammond City Council members told *The Times of Northwest Indiana* they were concerned about loitering, littering and other quality-of-life issues for residents. A nearby resident expressed concerns with fights and patrons urinating in neighbors' lawns, calling the club a "nuisance." The signage on the vacant nightclub remains.

Today, shopping options are limited to a Strack & Van Til, the It's Just Serendipity antique store and a few smaller stores. But the downtown is still home to a lot of activity, including law offices, the Towle Theatre, Paul Henry's Art Gallery, the South Shore Arts Substation No. 9, a business incubator, the 18th Street Brewery and Distillery and First Baptist Church's sprawling campus. Helmed by It's Just Serendipity owner and general dynamo Karen Maravilla, the Downtown Hammond Council aggressively promotes downtown Hammond with events like Arts on the Ave, a Polish Walking Pilgrimage Pole-looza and the annual Downtown Hammond Holiday Kick-Off Celebration, which doubles as a tribute to Hammond's own Jean Shepherd. The Beatles Fest and the Cold Roses Brew & Music Festival pack thousands downtown. But Lakeshore Chamber of Commerce president Dave Ryan estimated that as many as 300,000 square feet of space sit unused in the downtown. "I've seen so many master plans for the downtown area over the last 30 years," Redevelopment Commission Board member Louis Karubas told the *The Times of Northwest Indiana*. "I could write a book on them." Hammond recently turned to Jeff Speck, the author of

Walkable City: How Downtown Saves America, One Step at a Time, to get ideas for how to revitalize downtown.

"The core of the city is a little challenged, as is common with smaller cities across the country," Director of Economic Development Anne Anderson said. "We're bringing in Jeff Speck, an author and lecturer who's been all over the country looking at walkability, livability and creating spaces to walk around in. He's spent some time in downtown Hammond and loved it. He said it had great bones and many anchors vital to a downtown." His fellow planner David Dixon agreed that downtown Hammond's walkability could help lure new residents, especially with the possibility of a downtown South Shore Line station as part of the West Lake Corridor expansion. "If you want to envision the Hammond of the future, you ought to think more about what Hammond was like before 1950, rather than thinking about the Hammond that became like a suburb," Dixon said, according to the *Post-Tribune*. "It's almost like thinking about that movie, *Back to the Future*. If you think about the time between 1920 and 1940, this city was at its peak and to return to a peak, we're going to have to adopt many of the concepts of the past." Speck proposed multiple enhancements, including narrowing streets, adding bike lanes, planting more landscaping and locating a South Shore Line station downtown.

7

MOVIE THEATERS

Known as the "wonder theatre" and "Indiana's finest theatre," the vintage Parthenon Theatre opened at 5144 Hohman Avenue in 1921 with a capacity of 2,500, second only to the State Theater, which offered more than 3,000 seats to downtown moviegoers. O'Hern recalled in the Hammond Historical Society's *Pages from the Past* that it often screened "kissing-type movies." "We boys didn't care for that type of thing," O'Hern wrote. "We would go if Lon Chaney was there. We'd see these grand ushers. The big organ. They also had vaudeville shows and that was great. One time they had Rin Tin Tin on the stage with a *Rin Tin Tin* movie. After the movie he was in the lobby with his trainer and I walked up and touched him. That was a great experience for a boy." Warner Bros. brought the vintage movie theater to downtown Hammond as part of its original circuit outside of California. As O'Hern noted, it also hosted vaudeville shows and visiting celebrities, as well as big-band concerts, in those early days. "For a quarter in the late 1950s and early '60s, kids in Whiting, East Chicago and neighboring Illinois towns would catch a bus on Saturdays to the Parthenon Theatre in the heart of Hammond's bustling downtown and spend the afternoon watching a double-feature matinee," according to *The Times of Northwest Indiana*. "Often, instead of munching popcorn while they watched first-run motion pictures, some patrons would sneak in caramel corn from the Karmel Korn Shop, attached to the Paramount Theatre building."

The Neo–Italian Renaissance and Baroque-style theater hosted Douglas Fairbanks, Harry Houdini, Jack Benny and various big bands before

The Parthenon Theatre was one of the grandest in Hammond. *Hammond Public Library.*

converting to first-run films. It had a Kimball organ and a lavishly decorated lobby—complete with caged songbirds—that could accommodate more than one thousand people. "All the Parthenon Theatre's public areas were richly decorated, like a Renaissance-era princely palace, and furnished with the finest artwork and furniture, including caged songbirds in the main lobby," according to the Cinema Treasures website.

In the 1960s and 1970s, the Parthenon began to host concerts from musicians like Aerosmith and Sonny and Cher. In 1974, it hosted the Canadian band Rush, a prog rock act with a cult following, as an opening act for KISS. It was one of the few early KISS concerts that was videotaped and preserved for posterity. Northwest Indiana historian James Lane, a professor emeritus at Indiana University Northwest, remembered paying twenty dollars at the Parthenon to watch George Foreman challenge heavyweight champion Muhammad Ali in 1974 in the Rumble in the Jungle in Zaire. Attendees cheered and jeered and placed bets on the fight, which was streamed in directly through a closed circuit. "It brought out a lot of

LOST HAMMOND, INDIANA

EVENING PROGRAM
SOUSA AND HIS BAND

Lieut.-Commander JOHN PHILIP SOUSA, Conductor

HARRY ASKIN, *Manager*

Miss Nora Fauchald, *Soprano*   Mr. John Dolan, *Cornet*
Miss Rachel Senior, *Violin*   Mr. George Carey, *Xylophone*

1. Rhapsody, "The Indian" .... *Orem*
   Among those who have made careful records and researches of the music of the Aborigines of America may be named Thurlow Lieurance, Charles Cadman, and Arthur Farwell. The Indian themes introduced into this rhapsody were recorded by Mr. Lieurance and welded into rhapsodic form by the well-known composer, Preston Ware Orem.

2. Cornet Solo, "Cleopatra" .... *Demare*
   MR. JOHN DOLAN

3. Portraits, "At the King's Court" .... *Sousa*
   (a) "Her Ladyship, the Countess"
   (b) "Her Grace, the Duchess"
   (c) "Her Majesty, the Queen"

4. Soprano Solo, "The Lark Now Leaves His Wat'ry Nest" ...... *Parker*
   MISS NORA FAUCHALD

5. Fantasy, "The Victory Ball" .... *Schelling*
   This is Mr. Schelling's latest-completed work. The score bears the inscription: "To the memory of an American soldier." The fantasy is based on Alfred Noyes' poem, "The Victory Ball," herewith reprinted by permission from "The Elfin Artist and Other Poems" by Alfred Noyes. Copyright 1920, by Frederick A. Stokes Company.

   The cymbals crash, and the dancers walk,
   With long silk stockings and arms of chalk,
   Butterfly skirts, and white breasts bare,
   And shadows of dead men watching 'em there.

   Shadows of dead men stand by the wall,
   Watching the fun of the Victory Ball.
   They do not reproach, because they know,
   If they're forgotten, it's better so.

   Under the dancing feet are the graves.
   Dazzle and motley, in long bright waves,
   Brushed by the palm-fronds, grapple and whirl
   Ox-eyed matron and slim white girl.

   See, there is one child fresh from school,
   Learning the ropes as the old hands rule.
   God, how that dead boy gapes and grins
   As the tom-toms bang and the shimmy begins.
   "What did you think we should find," said a shade,
   "When the last shot echoed and the peace was made?"
   "Christ," laughed the fleshless jaws of his friend,
   "I thought they'd be praying for worlds to mend."
   "Pish," said a statesman standing near,
   "I'm glad they can busy their thoughts elsewhere!
   We mustn't reproach them. They're wrong, you see."
   Ah, said the dead men, "so were we!"

   Victory! Victory! On with the dance!
   Back to the jungle the new beasts prance!
   God, how the dead men grin by the wall,
   Watching the fun of the Victory Ball!

INTERVAL

6. Caprice, "On With the Dance" .... *Strung together by Sousa*
   Being a medley of famous tunes

7. (a) Xylophone Solo, "Nocturne and Waltz" .... *Chopin*
   MR. GEORGE CAREY

   (b) March, "Nobles of the Mystic Shrine" (new) .... *Sousa*

8. Violin Solo, "Faust Fantasia" .... *Sarasate*
   MISS RACHEL SENIOR

9. Folk Tune, "Country Gardens" .... *Grainger*

Encores will be selected from the following compositions and arrangements of John Philip Sousa: Semper Fidelis, Blue Danube, King Cotton, High School Cadets, The Glory of the Yankee Navy, Mr. Gallagher and Mr. Shean, Comrades of the Legion, U. S. Field Artillery, The Stars and Stripes Forever, Humoresque of "The Silver Lining" from "Sally", March of the Wooden Soldiers, Rameses, El Capitan, Washington Post, The Gallant Seventh, The Fairest of the Fair.

John Philip Sousa performed at the Parthenon Theatre in downtown Hammond. *Calumet Regional Archives.*

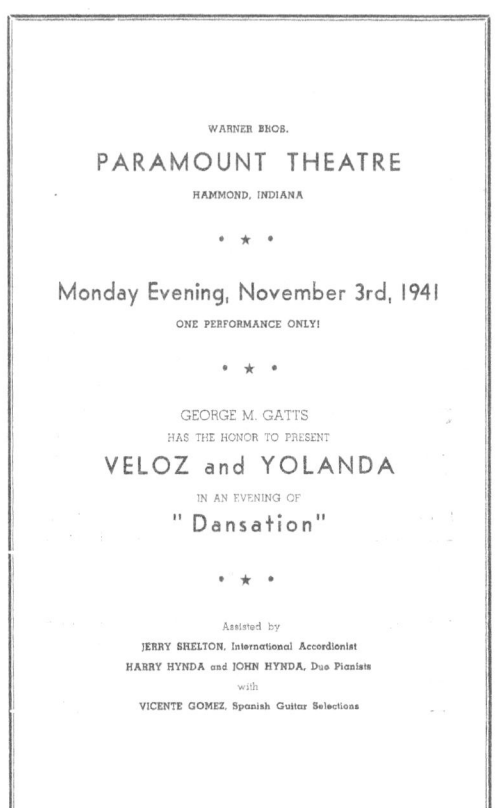

The famed ballroom dance duo Frank Veloz and Yolanda Casazza performed at the Paramount Theatre in 1941. *Hammond Public Library.*

boxing fans," he said. "It was a rope-a-dope fight in which Ali absorbed all these punches and looked like he was getting killed by Foreman, but tired him out and knocked him out in the eighth or ninth round. As I recall, they showed a softcore porno right before the fight." Even near the end, the Parthenon was a sight to behold, Lane said. "It was a grand old theater with great detail as was the Palace Theatre (in Gary) and many theaters in those days. It was a big grand old place, as were most of the buildings built in that era." The longest-lasting last grand movie palace left standing the Hammond, the Parthenon Theatre finally closed in the early 1980s after displaying a plaintive request to "shop downtown" on its marquee. A nearby billboard claimed Hammond "had everything: value, variety and parking." The vintage movie palace was demolished for good in 1983.

TOWLE OPERA HOUSE

Marcus M. Towle, one of Hammond's founders, built the city's second opera house in 1903, opening the Towle Opera House at the southeast corner of Hohman Avenue and Sibley. In the early twentieth century, the opera playhouse was *the* destination for culture and entertainment. "The Towle Opera House was by far the most modern to date and the best equipped of any in the city," stated an article on the Hammond High School Class of 1959 history website. "It was generally referred to as Hammond's leading playhouse. The Towle Opera House often showcased the best attractions available in the Region. In fact, they were on par with the first-class theaters in Chicago." The Towle Opera House and was later rebranded as the Hammond Theatre, the De Lux Theatre and finally the Deluxe Theatre, a movie house, before it was ultimately torn down in 1928 to make way for a department store that was turned into a Woolworth's 5 & 10, a staple of most American cities at the time. O'Hern recalled the Deluxe Theatre as "something special." His father took him and his two siblings to shows there on Sunday afternoons so their mother "could have a little peace and quiet." "We would ride the streetcar all the way down Columbia to Conkey, Conkey to Hohman, and Hohman to the Deluxe Theatre," he wrote. "We saw a lot of great shows. One was Douglas Fairbanks in *Ali Baba and the Forty Thieves*. I still remember him jumping out of those big jars. Another was Colleen Moore in *Peter Pan*. The dog stole the show. It must have been a man dressed as a dog."

THE STATE THEATRE

If the Towle went out with a whimper, the State Theatre went out with a bang. The State Theatre was famously bombed in 1927 in a blast that could be heard across Hammond, rousing many sleeping residents. "The beauty and grandeur of the State Theatre now laid in ruins," the Hammond Historical Society said in its *Flashback* newsletter. "Its stateliness as the state's most luxurious movie palace was short lived, just 15 months from its opening until the bombing." The theater was built at 556 State Street at the intersection of Sibley Street, and "no expense was spared," including on air conditioning, still a rarity at the time. It cost $1.7 million, or more than $24.5 million in today's dollars, and was the biggest movie theater in Indiana at the time. "It was declared 'One of the World's Wonder Theatres,'" noted the *Flashback* newsletter. "It was indeed stately from its fine quarried Italian marble columns and floors, to brass and crystal lighting fixtures and Italian walnut paneling."

Built by brothers William and Andrew Karzas, the duo behind the Aragon Ballroom in Chicago, the State Theatre was so lavish the famous *American Magazine* illustrator Allen Weary visited the theater the week before it opened, spending entire days sketching the magnificent interior views of the palatial auditorium. The Bryant Galleries in Chicago showcased his drawings in a special exhibit. "It will prove an inspiration to the entire community and an everlasting monument to the commercial and social progress made by the city during the period in which it was built," an August 25, 1926 story in *The Hammond Times* said.

There was much fanfare after Hammond landed a posh movie palace considered comparable to those in some of America's biggest cities, rivaling deluxe theaters in New York City and Chicago, where Hammond residents allegedly would no longer need to venture for entertainment. Its opening in August 1926 was celebrated with three days of festivities that included vaudeville, dancing, a twelve-piece band and what was then the largest fireworks display in city history. The streets were packed with pedestrians for the grand opening when the Italian Renaissance theater showed Buster Keaton's silent film *The Battering Butler*. It also showed talkies and hosted live performances, according to *The Times*.

"What a beautiful building it was," O'Hern wrote in the Hammond Historical Society's *Pages from the Past*.

> *I was in a classroom right across the street when it was going up. We were supposed to be doing our schoolwork there at All Saints, but we could also look out the window and watch the workmen. I was so fascinated, not so much by the bricklayers, but by the riveters. One fellow would get a rivet red hot in a little store and throw it maybe forty or fifty feet to the fellow doing the actual riveting who would catch it with a little cup. They never missed. I'd think what if he missed and one of those red-hot rivets would go down someone's back.*

The Karzas brothers billed the 3,500-seat State Theatre as "by far the largest and most daring amusement enterprise ever attempted in the theatrical history in the country." By all accounts, it was incredibly opulent. Designed by architect Walter J. Alschlager of Chicago and built by Longacre

Construction of New York, the Italian Renaissance movie palace featured seven hundred tons of structural steel, massive Italian marble Corinthian columns, leather-upholstered opera-style chairs, Grecian urns, hand-painted murals, an Italian walnut–paneled balcony, a bronze and marble ticket kiosk and black and gold marble floors. The theater had bronze fixtures, a terra-cotta façade, the second-floor Granada Ballroom for dancing and other festivities and a $50,000 Kimball organ that would have cost more than $683,000 today.

As *The Times* wryly noted in a 2016 article, the "extremely short-lived" theater "went out with a bang" just seventeen months after it opened. At about 1:50 a.m. on November 8, 1927, a blast rocked the city. "Fireman Ed Olejniczak, working at No. 1's station was knocked out of his bed as were many Hammond residents," Gordon D. Whitney wrote in the Hammond Historical Society's *History of the Hammond, Indiana Fire Department*. "Within seconds the fire department switchboard began to light up with calls. It didn't take long for the boys from No. 1 to arrive on the scene, shortly followed by the No. 4 crew." But when they arrived, it was too late. "What once had been the most beautiful showplace in Hammond and considered by many of the largest theatre in the entire state, now lay in ruins," Whitney lamented. "It seemed almost incredible that there was little or no fire and that little was quickly extinguished by the engine's booster hose. The entire front of the building facing State Street was blown out. It had opened in 1926 at a cost of $2 million and with a seating capacity of over 3,000. Although it was covered extensively by insurance, it was not covered for bombing."

Miraculously, no one was injured in the blast that laid the theater completely to waste, causing plaster to fall onto sleeping residents across the city. The explosion blew out large sections of the wall and roof, filling the street with bricks, severely damaging All Saints Church across the street and blocking the Gary Railway Company's trolley tracks. "The person had evidently watched the late show that night and left a satchel with two sticks of dynamite and a mercury switch, which he activated as he was leaving," Hammond Public Library local history librarian Richard Lytle told *The Times*. "So consequently the theater was cleared of everybody but the janitor when this mercury switch timer went off. Now the only person in the theater at the time was the janitor, and it blew him straight across the street. It blew out windows all around, including the All Saints rectory, which was across the street to the south."

The cause of the bombing was never officially known. Chicago newspapers speculated that a fanatic was irate that it sat across from the All

Saints Church. Others put forward theories that one of many rival movie theaters sought to put it out of business, possibly the Bijou Photoplay Theatre just two blocks down State Street—since there was much fierce competition—or that it was a mob hit at a time when gangsters like Al Capone and John Dillinger ran wild. O'Hern, an altar boy at All Saints across the street, witnessed the devastation firsthand: "At 7 a.m. the morning after the theater was blown up, I came walking down here and saw this horrible mess. That beautiful theater was just devastated. The roof was blown off, sides blown out, and trash all over the street. I looked at the school and every window was broken. I didn't know what to do. The church was above the school and there was debris all over the place. Right on the altar was a piece of the panic bar. I just started trying to put the sanctuary back in order." Theater operator William Kleihege was later charged with plotting the bombing to file an insurance claim after he could no longer afford the lease payments, paying projectionist Joseph Million $2,000 to plant dynamite, according to *The Times*. Both men were convicted, but the Indiana Supreme Court set aside Kleihege's conviction and he was eventually cleared of all charges in 1934.

The bombing struck a blow to Hammond's civic pride. "It broke our hearts," O'Hern wrote in *Pages from the Past*. "We had been so proud of the State Theatre. It was the most modern and beautiful theater in the whole Region at that time when sound movies began to be shown." The badly damaged building was repurposed to host an A&P Grocery Store, a roller-skating rink, a furniture store and a Laundromat. "After the bombing there was talk of rebuilding the theater, however that never did materialize," according to the Hammond Historical Society's newsletter. "Over time the theatre succumbed to the elements and vandals." The iconic vertical marquee, which once towered over and electrified downtown Hammond, came down in 1947 when it started to become unstable. Two decades later, the last remnants of the splendid State Theatre were demolished in 1967 to make way for a new Hammond Public Library building.

THE BIJOU PHOTOPLAY

In the early days of Hammond, the many rival theaters brought a variety of movies as well as theater, opera and vaudeville acts to downtown Hammond. "Developing cities in the United States were proud to display the entertainment offerings of their community in an attempt to show that their city had a lot of culture and was a good place to live," an article on the Hammond High School Class of 1959 webpage stated. "This attracted residents to the area." The Bijou at 173 State Street originally brought vaudeville and silent film to the area. The Van Sickle family owned and operated the theater from 1909 across from the Edward C. Minas department store. The owners installed a piano-organ in 1913 and later an electric projection machine. Around town, it was called the "Bi-jo." "I guess it was supposed to be the Bijou, which is French for jewel," O'Hern wrote in *Pages from the Past*.

> *This is where we saw William S. Hart, the greatest cowboy actor of all time. I remember one scene where he sat on his horse outside a saloon and threw his lariat over the swinging doors, lasoed [sic] three bad guys standing at the bar and dragged them into the street. They also had the serials where they would always leave the hero running into a buzzsaw, falling under the wheels of a train, and so forth. You had to go back the next week to see what happened to him.*

THE ORPHEUM THEATRE

The Orpheum Theatre opened as a vaudeville house on East State Street in downtown Hammond in 1912, making it one of Hammond's earliest theaters, according to the Cinema Treasures website. The *Hammond Times* reported that Peter and Mary Schutz built the four-story, 850-seat Orpheum for $80,000, a princely sum for the time. Early performers included Fred Allen, Jack Benny, Eddie Foy, various dramatic stock companies, the "celebrated" (but widely heckled) Cherry Sisters and the four Marx brothers, who performed the musical tabloid *Fun in Hi Skule* there. Groucho Marx smoked his huge cigar on stage in downtown Hammond long before his quick wit won him renown on the radio, on Broadway and in movies. Allen juggled, and Benny played violin before riveted audiences. A lightweight champion and former heavyweight champion boxed on the dance hall on the fourth floor.

Billed as "Hammond's most beautiful playhouse" and home to "high-class vaudeville and musical attractions," the spacious theater with an orchestra pit and a balcony lost some luster in the 1920s when larger and more ornate movie palaces were constructed, including the State Theatre, the Parthenon Theatre and the Paramount Theatre. The Orpheum staged plays daily. "Twice a week they changed plays," O'Hern wrote in *Pages from the Past*. "How could they do that! For several years they had stage plays. They had the same cast, the leading man, the leading woman, the old man, the dowager, the ingenue, the comic relief actor, and for about two years they put on two plays each week." The Orpheum switched over to movies in 1921 as fashions changed and Hollywood's magic captured the public imagination. Warner Bros. Circuit Management Corporation took it over by 1941, after which it screened many World War II submarine flicks.

It closed in the early 1952, going on to have a date with the wrecking ball. "There are many ghosts in the darkened Orpheum Theater—ghosts that dance and sing and act as they once did in real life," a *Hammond Times* article in the early 1950s said. "And the ghosts are not all human for some are seals, dogs and even the trained birds of vaudeville." Though long ago demolished, the Orpheum was immortalized by Hammond's own creative genius Jean Shepherd in the story "Leopold Doppler and the Great Orpheum Gravy Boat Riot." First published in *Playboy Magazine* and later in the short story collection *In God We Trust, All Others Pay Cash*, the humorous story recounts how Orpheum manager Leopold Doppler boosted the sluggish attendance during the Great Depression by luring more women into matinees with promises of cheap dinnerware.

Catastrophe ensued when dinner plates did not arrive on schedule, and he was forced to hand out gravy boats instead. The quick-thinking Doppler placated the angry crowd of women by telling them to return the next week when they could trade in the gravy boats for the more desirable plates. The next week, the plate had still not arrived, and he had to step out on stage at intermission to appease the increasingly agitated crowd with the same story. After four weeks, they were no longer buying it. He claimed there had been another mix-up in the shipment, and it turned into a scene straight out of *Animal House*.

"Then it happened," Shepherd wrote. "A dark shadow sliced through the hot beam of the spotlight, turning over and over and casting upon the screen an enormous magnified outline of a great Gravy Boat. Spinning over and over, it crashed with a startling suddenness on the stage at Doppler's feet. Instantly a blizzard of Gravy Boats filled the air." Doppler protested for calm, but to no avail. "A great crash of Gravy Boats like the breaking surf on an alien shore drowned out his words," Shepherd wrote. "And then, spreading to all corners of the house, shopping bags were emptied as the arms rose and fell in the darkness, maniacal female cackles and obscenities driving Doppler from the stage."

HOHMAN THEATER

Though not Hammond's shortest-lived movie theater, the Hohman Theater didn't make it to the end of its twenty-year lease. The one-screen, one-thousand-seat movie house was designed by architect L. Cosby Bernard and built for $65,000. It opened on Christmas Day in 1936 with a showing of *Laughing Irish Eyes*. The building was later repurposed to host Citizens Financial Bank, which was acquired by Muncie-based First Merchants for $140 million in 2013. First Merchants remodeled the building in 2016 to include a drive-through and office space for the not-for-profit Mental Health America of Lake County.

THE PARAMOUNT THEATRE

The Paramount Theatre at 5405 Hohman Avenue a few blocks from the Parthenon Theatre could seat nearly two thousand when it opened in 1930. The one-screen theater showed movies and hosted live stage shows from performers like Minnie Pearl, Pat Boone and the Benny Goodman Band, according to Cinema Treasures. Legends like Bob Hope and Bing Crosby performed there. The Paramount was not as ornate as the Pantheon or State, but it rolled out the red carpet for moviegoers. There was a uniformed doorman, and ushers whisked patrons to their seats. A house orchestra provided musical accompaniment to the movies. The Paramount also featured live stage shows as late as the 1950s, according to *The Times*, which described it as smaller but equally lovely as the Parthenon. In 1965, the British Invasion sensation the Dick Clark Five drew of crowd of two thousand "frantically screaming, mostly female fans." Some of the die-hard fans arrived at 3:00 a.m. Friday morning for the appearance, which was in conjunction with a screening of the movie *Catch Us If You Can*. More than six hundred people were turned away from the sold-out event.

But the crowds eventually thinned. After falling into disrepair for decades, the Paramount was closed for good in 1981 and razed two years later. One last effort was made to revive the landmark to its former glory in the late 1980s. Two investors purchased the property for what they thought was a bargain price of $100, not realizing they were on the hook for $25,000 in back taxes. They also discovered the theater was in much worse condition than it appeared from the outside, with plaster falling from the ceiling and

Veloz and Casazza once appeared at the Paramount Theatre. *Hammond Public Library.*

two-foot hole in the roof, Linda Perunko wrote in *Steel Shavings*. That alone would have cost $100,000 to fix. "In the spring of 1988, Steve and Don asked me to help them tear out seats," she wrote. "They wanted to sell the metal to raise money which they were low on. Trouble hit again in the summer of 1988. St. Margaret's Hospital wanted to buy the land to build a parking lot. Unfortunately, Steve and Don did not own the land. Furthermore, a problem was found in the contract, and nobody was sure who actually owned the building. This problem had to be settled in court." Plitt Entertainment won the court case and sold off the property. After providing generations with cinematic magic, the Paramount had one final hurrah. "The lights of the marquee burned one last time on Saturday, December 8, 1990," Perunko added. "A couple of area men lit the marquee with a generator before the building was scheduled to be torn down."

KENNEDY THEATRE

Not all Hammond's grand movie theaters were downtown. After entertaining neighborhood kids for nearly eighty years, the "rocking chair theatre" in Hammond's Hessville neighborhood showed its final reel in 2015, finally falling victim to the suburban multiplexes. A fading *Mockingjay* poster still hangs up outside the movie theater, which opened as the Hess in 1937 and was also known as the Ace. The two-screen movie house, which could seat around six hundred in high-backed rockers, was renamed after President John F. Kennedy in 1963. The sign had a silhouette of President Kennedy's rocking chair, which relieved his chronic back pain. At that time, the Kennedy Theatre mainly showed second-run double features. Then *Jaws* swam into the theater, running for six months and ushering in a new era in which the Kennedy became a first-run theater that showed many movies exclusive to Northwest Indiana. But hard times struck in the 1980s, to the point where it could no longer advertising showtimes in both *The Hammond Times* and the *Post-Tribune*. It closed in 1996 but was remodeled by cutting the theater in half so it had two screens of about two hundred seats each, including one with an upstairs skybox with twenty-two seats where viewers could get unlimited popcorn and soda delivered to them for a higher-priced ticket. The Kennedy closed again in 2001 but reopened the next year when two new families acquired it.

They took down a brick wall with a portrait of President Kennedy across from the box office and concession counter and replaced it with mirrors. They showed many family-friendly films that catered to neighborhood kids who just walked over, including *The Incredibles*, *Shrek 2* and entries from the Harry Potter series. With tickets as low as five dollars and popcorn that started at two, it still sometimes drew lines down the street for big releases but only attracted three or four moviegoers for some screenings of duds like *The Lone Ranger*. Plans to expand by buying the arthouse Town Theatre in Highland fell apart when the town government snapped that property up in a tax sale and sat on it until it deteriorated to the point where it had to be demolished. The Kennedy closed again in 2015 after the owners failed to raise enough funds to switch it from the old 35mm film reels to digital projection. Major studios nationwide stopped sending out the more expensive 35mm reels, which forced many one-screen theaters out of business because of the steep $60,000 to $70,000 cost of a digital projector. *Indiewire* estimated as many as one thousand independent cinemas faded to black nationwide.

8
DEPARTMENT STORES

E.C. MINAS

A fixture for more than a century that was known for its exceptional customer service, the E.C. Minas Department Store on Hohman in downtown Hammond was developed by Edward C. Minas, the mogul who built a Tudor Revival mansion on Forest Avenue around 1930. The Wabash College graduate, Crown Point native and MM Towle Store clerk earned a master's degree in business administration at Indiana University–Bloomington and started a hardware store in 1890s before running the vaunted department store downtown. He led the campaign to bring the YMCA to Hammond and was named Jaycees Man of the Year. The Hammond Historical Society described him in *The Famous 1904 Edition of the Hammond Daily News* as "One of Hammond's Youngest Businessmen But Every Inch a Hustler." He started his department store business—sometimes called the Marshall Field's of Hammond—in 1894 and it lasted until 1984, more than half a century after his death.

Minas originally opened a hardware store on State and Oakley that made $2.62 its first day. The three-story building, originally lit by kerosene lamps, offered the first store-owned parking lot in Hammond and later built the city's largest parking garage. "The significant building era of this designation ran from 1885 to 1915, during which time the Minas building was constructed," then–city planner Brian Poland told *The Times of Northwest Indiana*. "The second significant time period was from 1920 to 1927, that pre-Depression boom when other buildings on State Street were constructed." During the

E.C. Minas was a longstanding Hammond institution. *Hammond Public Library.*

Roaring Twenties, the Minas Furniture Company took over a five-story building at State Street and Oakley Avenue. The building by Chicago architect Leon F. Urbane featured new ideas in terra-cotta design and devoted all five floors to the display of furniture. The Minas department store was an elegant place where employees wrapped the gifts and elevator operators wore white gloves. The store deployed many sales tactics, offering coupons and trading stamps, placing umbrellas out on the sidewalks, painting ads on the sides of barns outside of town and busing visitors in from area hamlets with promises of free lunch. "Newspaper advertising became an important contact to the public early in the history of the store, even before the turn of the century." Hammond Historical Society secretary Majorie Sohl wrote in the *Tales from the Past.* "Most business was on a cash basis, but early ledgers contain the names of most of the early families in the area. First deliveries were made by wheelbarrow, later by wagons, and then by trucks."

Minas was known as the "store with a heart" that provided "service and satisfaction to its customers." Lighting up downtown Hammond with bright neon lights, it bragged it was the city's "oldest and finest department store."

E.C. Minas was one of downtown Hammond's most beloved department stores. *Hammond Public Library.*

"As you walked through the revolving door at Minas's, you would be greeted with a friendly, genuine smile from the nearest Minas employee," Hammond native Tom Johnson wrote for the Hammond High School Class of 1959 history website. "In the summertime, passing through that revolving door would be like going through the Pearly Gates. You had immediate relief from the sweltering heat of the street, and in the soothing, cool air of the store was a heavenly scent that defied description. What was the source of those wonderful scents that wafted through the ancient department stores in those days?" He remembered how the Minas store had an elevator with an operator. "The operator wore white gloves and always had a warm smile for you. She would always be polite and professional in her demeanor," Johnson wrote. "You always felt that you were appreciated as a customer at the Edward C. Minas Store. Minas's carried quality merchandise and offered it at a fair price. You could find items cheaper at other stores, but you would be compromising on quality by buying them instead of the Minas merchandise."

Minas was one of the biggest draws downtown. "The 400 block of State Street, the home of Minas', was probably equally as prestigious as the 5200

E.C. Minas and Goldblatt's were the long the local retail anchors of downtown Hammond. *Hammond Public Library.*

block of Hohman," Johnson wrote. "Minas' was the flagship establishment of that block, but there were other large stores as well." E.C. Minas died in 1949, but the family-owned business he established carried on, adding air conditioning and an insurance plan for employees over the next few years.

E.C. Minas started out as a hardware store in 1890. *Hammond Public Library.*

But all things eventually come to an end. Minas, Goldblatt's, Rothschild's, York, Spiegel's, Woolworth's, JCPenney, Montgomery Ward and S.S. Kresge, the predecessor of Kmart, all had department stores in downtown Hammond back before it began to start to decline in the 1960s. They increasingly fell out of favor as the Woodmar Mall opened in Hammond in the 1950s, the 1.3-million-square-foot River Oaks Center opened in neighboring Calumet City in the 1960s and the super-regional Southlake Mall opened in Hobart in the 1970s. The number of retail stores in all of Hammond fell from 752 in 1972 to just 332 in 2002, according to the *Gary Post-Tribune*. Shoppers fled to the suburbs, and some of the stores even relocated, leaving the downtown behind to the point where all that remains of its retail heyday is the golden Goldblatt's clock hanging in the stairwell of the downtown Hammond Public Library.

In the 1990s, there was an effort to convert the old department store building into the State Street Lofts, which would have featured fourteen-foot ceilings, exposed brick walls and duct work, Corinthian counters and Jacuzzi hot tubs. "This building, which housed the most elegant department store of its time,

E.C. Minas was a popular shopping destination in downtown Hammond. *Hammond Public Library.*

catered to society's elite, from the flapper set of the Roaring Twenties through both world wars. It was indisputably Hammond's most famous landmark," according to the Hammond Historical Society's *Flashback* newsletter.

> *The proposed development was to feature 15 retail/office loft condominiums located on the first floor and 22 residential loft condominiums located on the second and third floors. The residences were to be superior in construction to their Chicago counterparts, offer more amenities, and are often one-half to one-third the price. The project would have signaled the first phase of a gentrification plan for the creation of a professional haven and arts district among the classic architecture located on State Street. Also planned were future sites of famous Chicago restaurants, galleries and coffee houses all to be locates within walking distance of the State Street Lofts.*

None of that, of course, ever came to fruition.

The then-108-year-old Minas building was torn down in 2002 after the terra-cotta façade was removed to make way for a new First Baptist Church auditorium. The church planned to spend up to $15 million on a new four-story auditorium that would seat up to 5,500. "The new building will be twice as big as the Minas building," then–city planner Brian Poland told *The Times*. "Saving the facade was an expensive proposition, and so is demolishing that building." Minas's legacy lives on with the Munster-based South Shore Arts League that operates galleries in Hammond, Munster and Crown Point and has educated countless Region residents on how to paint, draw, sculpt and pursue countless other artistic disciplines. A drawing of a hat from Minas's famous hat department served as the South Shore Art League's logo. The annual exhibit of regional artists from across Indiana and Cook County, Illinois, began in the Minas hat department in 1936 after Marshall Field's in downtown Chicago ended its annual Hoosier Salon show, forcing the artists to turn to the department store in Hammond as a replacement venue.

JCPENNEY

Another longtime anchor of Hammond's retail hub, JCPenney moved across Hohman Avenue to the northeast corner of Hohman and Sibley Street in the 1960s, just as the downtown started to decline and discount shops moved in. It was replaced at its original location by an Army/Navy War Surplus Store. The abandoned department store was demolished in 2016 with the help of U.S. Department of Housing and Urban Development funds after city officials determined that water damage kept it from being rehabbed, as it had standing water in it for many years. The lot remains empty today.

WOOLWORTH'S

After the Deluxe Theater was demolished, it was replaced with a Woolworth's five-and-dime, which at one point was the largest department store chain in the world. One could grab a meal for less than a dollar in the luncheonette. "It was the original Walmart of its time," an article on the Hammond High School Class of 1959 webpage stated. "Our Woolworth store was great for reviewing the latest comic books, buying goldfish in a paper box, or meeting your friends at the lunch counter and sharing the most recent gossip." The Woolworth's occupied a three-story building on Hohman Avenue with a wide

Woolworth's was a popular hangout in downtown Hammond. *Hammond Public Library.*

wooden staircase and creaking hardwood floors. "Woolworth's provided jobs for teenagers and early training for careers in hospitality, cooking, public relations, retail sales counter, everything a young woman would need to know to make her a successful housewife," the article continued. "After all, it was the 1950s, and if you were a teenager you had to have a job. What better job could you have than one that would allow you time to meet your classmates, chat with your neighbors, meet new boys and—the best part—you could help yourself to a free coke."

Hammond native Tom Johnson remembered on the Class of 1959 website that downtown was once central to social life in the city. "Walgreens and Woolworth's had lunch counters that served burgers, fries and fountain drinks," he wrote. "Downtown was much more than just a place to shop: it was a place where friends met to have lunch, or to take in a movie, or to just 'hang out.'" It was such a cornucopia of plenty it was worth visiting for the window shopping alone. "Ah Woolworth's," O'Hern wrote:

What a paradise for just walking up and down the aisles and seeing hundreds of things priced at five and ten cents. Needles, pins, marbles, caps, thimbles, pencils, tablets, nails, wire, threat, kitchen utensils, knives, forks, dishes and toys, toys, toys. How we would walk up and down the aisles. A special kind of enjoyment was walking around the huge candy counter and just looking—as we seldom had the price of a dime's worth of candy. That did not stop us from enjoying the displays. There must have been hundreds of items displayed on the counters. One that sticks in my mind was the display box for "gold" rimmed spectacles. People would come in and stand at the counter and try on pair after pair of these spectacles. When they found the pair that did the best for them a purchase would be made.

LION STORE

Kaufman and Wolf boasted in the early 1900s that the Lion Store was Indiana's largest department store. It had two hundred feet of coveted frontage along Hohman Avenue at the busy intersection of Hohman and Rimbach. So pretty it was featured on postcards, the store sold stamps, prescription drugs and sundry other items. But the once resplendent shopping destination lasted only a few decades. "The owners of the Lion Store rebuilt the store in the late 1920s just in time to be clobbered by the Great Depression," O'Hern wrote in the Hammond Historical Society's *Pages from the Past*. "The owners, Kaufman and Wolf, had to give up their beautiful store. You can still see the initials K&W on the decorative terrazzo stones on the front of the building."

GOLDBLATT'S

Goldblatt Brothers of Chicago, which was founded in 1914 by the brothers Nate and Maurice Goldblatt, bought the Lion Store in downtown Hammond and renamed it Goldblatt's. A beloved local institution forever immortalized in Jean Shepherd's *A Christmas Story*, the towering Goldblatt's was the heart and soul of downtown Hammond. It was central to city life in a way few stores are anymore. "There probably is no way to appropriately pay tribute to the presence and history of the Goldblatt's Department Store in downtown

Goldblatt's was a downtown Hammond staple that was immortalized in *A Christmas Story*. *Hammond Public Library.*

Hammond, Indiana," an article on the Hammond High School Class of 1959 webpage asserted. "The four-story retail department store, complete with a lower-level basement, was the largest retail department store in the state of Indiana and had everything that the public could possibly want in a department store." Goldblatt's was known for the water tower on its roof, its unique bell system for summoning employees from throughout its floors and of course its Christmas window displays filled with many toys young boys and girls coveted. It also drew huge crowds to its basement meat market and deli, which hawked "blue ribbon beef," ham and many other specialties. Hammond residents still recall flocking there for hot dogs, patty melts, shakes and its famed cottage cheese. "Once your first visual impression made it past the rows of tripe, beef tongue, kidneys and heart, all laid out uncovered on metal trays, you began to realize that beyond the fragrances of fresh slaughter, there was a wonderful aroma of baked bread," a contributor to the Hammond High School Class of 1959 webpage stated. "Samples were rarely, if ever, served since everyone who shopped there knew what everything actually tasted like. But food items were openly displayed without protective cover. Home freezers were not available among the working class so fresh meats were purchased daily. What was left over was ground into sausage for sale the following day."

The Goldblatt's in Hammond was frequented by babushkas, headscarf-wearing Polish matrons and grandmothers who saw it as a place to socialize. The discount chain had as many as twenty stores in Chicago, Michigan, Wisconsin and Indiana, including in downtown Hammond and Gary. Shoppers could get everything: clothes, household items, deli food, meat and candy, according to *The Times*. But retailers like Sears, Kmart, Zayre and Woolco started to strip away market share in the mid-1960s as Hammond and the rest of the nation started to suburbanize.

Goldblatt's declared bankruptcy in 1981, rebounded after restructuring, and then started closing stores and selling the more viable ones to Ames in the 1990s, winding down the last of its operations in 2000. The Goldblatt's in downtown Hammond was demolished by implosion in 1994. Its Christmas display window and Santa visitation line live on, however, on cable television every holiday season during marathons of *A Christmas Story*, an adaptation of Jean Shepherd's book *In God We Trust, All Others Pay Cash* about growing up in Hammond. Shepherd himself played Santa in the movie, kicking his fictional stand-in Ralphie Parker down a slide after the boy couldn't recall what he wanted for Christmas and then, thwarted, rattled off that he wanted a Red Ryder BB gun.

"You'll shoot your eye out kid," he was one of many adults to intone during the collection of anecdotes. Hammond native Tom Johnson recalled on the Hammond High School Society of 1959 site that Goldblatt's helped make downtown an ideal place to walk around and window shop,

> *especially during the Christmas season, when all the city streets were adorned with decorations, and the store windows were alive with displays depicting scenes of the season. Some displays at Goldblatt's were even animated. It was so easy to feel the Christmas spirit when you walked around downtown Hammond, taking in all the decorations and displays with your breath steaming and your cheeks turned a rosy red from the crisp winter air. The sounds of Christmas music and the ringing of the Salvation Army Santa Claus's bell filled the air, and all around you were happy, smiling people doing their Christmas shopping.*

W.T. GRANT COMPANY

Just across the street from Goldblatt's, the W.T. Grant Company kept the comic books on the second floor to draw the kids in as much as possible. It was a national variety store chain typically located in downtowns that ran from 1906 to 1976, when it went bankrupt. W.T. Grant was perhaps best known for its lunch counters and its exclusive low-price Diva record label. An article on the *Hammond High School Class of 1959* webpage recalled how the wooden floors and steps of the mass merchandise store would squeak when you walked on them: "Goldfish were five cents and were put in a Chinese takeout box. They seldom survived the bus ride home and ended up unceremoniously being flushed down toilets throughout Hammond. 'Yard goods' did not refer to rakes and shovels. Many Hammond mothers still sewed their children's clothes and made their own dresses, guaranteeing return visits for 'yard goods' where you could buy fabric measured by the yard."

9
JEAN SHEPHERD'S HAMMOND

Hammond native Jean Shepherd, a 1939 graduate of Hammond High School, achieved cult status as a late-night radio host on the East Coast, celebrating his bohemian exploits in Greenwich Village on a New York City radio station with catchphrases like "excelsior" and pulling pranks like getting the nonexistent, wholly fabricated *I, Libertine* novel added to the *New York Times* bestseller list. He wrote short stories for *National Lampoon* and *Playboy Magazine* during the height of their cultural relevance, published books, toured the country for the *Jean Shepherd's America* show that aired on PBS and regaled late-night listeners of New York City's WOR along the Eastern Seaboard for decades with a show that was No. 1 among sixty-eight stations when he signed off in 1978. "It was so popular that there's a myth I was on all night—but it was a 45-minute show," Shepherd told the *South Florida Sun-Sentinel* in 1985. "Some nights I'd tell stories, play the kazoo—It was wild. It was a nightclub act, basically, on the radio. It had no format. I was the format." Hammond helped shape his radio persona, both by furnishing him with stories and by giving him a chance to hone his craft early on at WJOB. "I was born and raised in Hammond, Indiana, a steel town," he told the *Sun-Sentinel*. "And the first radio job I had was as a kid, I did the local game scores, 'cause I loved sports. I'd do a little commentary about the game. I realized the power of radio when people would come up to me and say, 'Boy, wait'll Roosevelt High hears what you said about them.'" The radio historian Max Schmid called the free-form improviser "the best man ever to sit before a microphone."

Shepherd immortalized Hammond in the best-selling classic *In God We Trust, All Others Pay Cash,* which was adapted into the holiday classic *A Christmas Story* that's played on loop on cable on Christmas Day. His crowning achievement depicts Hammond as "Hohman" and Goldblatt's as "Higbee's" in an idealized version of growing up in the city in the 1920s and 1930s. Goldblatt's is gone, save for the last vestige of an ornate clock hanging in the Hammond Public Library. The Warren J. Harding Elementary School, where Flick gets his tongue stuck to a flagpole and Ralphie is warned one of many times he would shoot his eye out, was torn down and rebuilt. The Cam-Lan Restaurant at 5256 Hohman Avenue that inspired the Peking duck decapitation scene after the Bumpus hounds make short work of the Yule turkey, which *A Native's Guide to Northwest Indiana* author Mark Skertic described as the "big Chinese restaurant in Hammond," long ago closed and was demolished.

Shepherd's relationship with his hometown could be conflicted, such as when some of his remarks about the Region during a talk at the main Lake County Public Library in Merrillville in the 1980s were taken as condescending. "Maybe the reason I don't come back to this town much is the minute I get out on Calumet Avenue I start to get a nervous feeling in my stomach," he said. "Right down the street is Hammond High. Some of the most hellish moments of my life took place there." Other derogatory remarks included "how would you like to start off life going to a school named after the worst president," in reference to Warren G. Harding Elementary School; "how many guys thought they would still be working at the steel mill for 300–400 years"; and the sarcastic "that's unassailable Indiana logic." He also remarked, "When I was growing up in Hammond, Merrillville was just a patch of cantaloupes surrounded by Kentucky hillbillies. Today, it's just a patch of cantaloupes."

The Hammond Shepherd immortalized in *A Christmas Story* is a faded memory. Ovaltine no longer commandeers the airwaves, capturing young kids' imaginations. Red Ryder BB guns have fallen out of fashion. Santa no longer drops in by helicopter at the Woodmar Mall to be interviewed by a reporter from WJOB. His depiction of an idyllic household life with his father, "the old man," and his mother, who was "always standing over the sink in a yellow rump-sprung chenille bathrobe with bits of dried egg on the label," is a world that no longer exists in Northwest Indiana and maybe never did. Though he was often accused of rose-tinted nostalgia, Shepherd did not hold back:

Peteyville in Hessville is perhaps Hammond's biggest annual celebration of Christmas. *Photo by author.*

Ours was not a genteel neighborhood, by any stretch of the imagination. Nestled picturesquely between the looming steel mills and the verminously aromatic oil refineries and encircled by a colorful conglomerate of city dumps and fetid rivers, our northern Indiana town was and is the very essence of the Midwestern industrial heartland of the nation. There was a standard barbershop bit of humor that said it with surprising poetism: If Chicago (only a stone's throw away across the polluted lake waters) was Carl Sandburg's "City of the Broad Shoulders," then Hohman had to be that city's broad rear end.

If the saccharine childhood idyll Shepherd often described has disappeared, so has the polluted wasteland he scorned. The Grand Calumet River, once so polluted even the sludge worms that feed on toxic waste could not survive there, has been cleaned up. Bald eagles now nest along the Little Calumet River. The steel mills now belch steam instead of smoke, and the dumps have been replaced by golf courses, parks and shopping centers.

10
HOTELS

INDIANA HOTEL

A Hammond landmark at Hohman Avenue and State Street that was demolished once and for all in 1992, the Indiana Hotel was known as a seedy place where kids shot billiards on pool tables in the smoky basement where the seasoned veterans rolled up packs of cigarettes into their T-shirt sleeves. "There were stories that Al Capone used to stay there after he toured his girly joints in Calumet City," stated an article on the *Hammond High School Class of 1959* site. "Perhaps this was an early indication of my sheltered existence as a kid." Hammond ordered that the building be vacated in 1990. Owner Richard Goodwin notified the 80 low-income tenants they would have to relocate. The hotel at 5116 Hohman Avenue had 20 employees, 103 rooms and a coin-operated laundry. The city razed it to make room for a railroad overpass at Hohman Avenue near State Street. The city also demolished the Army/Navy War Surplus Store at 5134 Hohman Avenue for the sake of that project.

GRAND HOTEL LASALLE

The Grand Hotel LaSalle also no longer exists, though its hand-painted sign still towers over the modest downtown Hammond skyline. Both glamorous and shady over the course of its long history, the Grand Hotel

Hammond bought and closed the Grand Hotel LaSalle, a longtime institution, in 2017. The city's oldest hotel had become a haven for the homeless. *Photo by author.*

LaSalle at 5266 Hohman Avenue dated to 1908, outlasting the department stores and movie palaces built around the same time. "It's not a big, fancy, modern hotel," *The Times* staff writer Doug Ross wrote. "Not all of the rooms have their own bathrooms. The LaSalle Hotel is for people who plan to spend a week or more, not overnight travelers. These tenants aren't high rollers." The Hotel LaSalle did host a baron and baroness from Norway in the early 1970s. It had a restaurant, a banquet room, brass handrails, a manually operated elevator and tunnels used by gangers to escape police during Prohibition. The walls were decorated with moose antlers, the heads of horned sheep and the replica of an Easter Island statue. The five-story hotel, originally a granary, was converted into a hotel called the Hotel Meade that hosted railroad workers and those who moved to the fledgling industrial city in search of work. An old switchboard was rigged into a system for sending wakeup calls and notifying residents they had visitors down in the lobby.

The Hotel LaSalle's Coffee Shop restaurant was decorated with more than a dozen newspaper front pages about historic events like Lincoln's assassination and the sinking of the *Titanic*. The gift shop was furnished with dolls, trinkets and other items from the Marshall Field's at the River Oaks Center in neighboring Calumet City. Hammond's Redevelopment Commission acquired the hotel for $700,000 in 2018. It became home to a transient population of about fifty long-term tenants the city asked to move as the city looked to repurpose the building, which Hammond Chief of Staff Phil Taillon told *The Times* will "definitely not be a hotel in the future." Some tenants had lived there as long as thirty-five years. Some were sex offenders referred there by the Indiana Department of Correction, one killed two women and many were poor. A forty-two-year-old man with mental problems and on disability hanged himself off a fire escape there in 2003, according to *Times* archives.

Lou Karubas owned the hotel for more than four decades. "Single light bulbs hanging from cords lit the long hallways," no light switches were in the room and there were no showers when he acquired it in the 1970s, according to *The Times of Northwest Indiana* archives. "They had no furniture and no linen," Karubas told *The Times*. "I met with the 12 stockholders in Room 505 with the lawyers and we couldn't find enough chairs in the hotel so everyone could sit down. The owners were old-timers and just couldn't keep the building up." He renovated the building with auction-bought items like marble tile, hanging glass light fixtures, a walnut desk in the lobby with stationery slots and spots for inkwells and a mirror with a carved wooden frame from the Pierson Hotel in Chicago.

Karubas beat city hall in 2001 when Hammond tried to impose a $5 registration fee per tenant. Tenants in 2008 paid as little as $400 a month for rent, with many sharing hallway bathrooms. Some tenants got referred there by St. Joseph's and the First Baptist Churches. "It's close to the church, to Strack & Van Til, to the soup line at St. Joseph Church, to Wendy's and Popeyes and to the library," Karubas told *The Times of Northwest Indiana*. "You don't have to have a car here." In its effort to clean up downtown and invite more redevelopment, the City of Hammond also acquired and razed the Jefferson Hotel in downtown Hammond in 2018.

THE JEFFERSON HOTEL

Less distinguished and storied than the Grand Hotel LaSalle, the three-story Jefferson dated back to 1919. The hotel at 415 West Sibley Street stood next to the former JCPenney department store Hammond tore down just a few years earlier. The Jefferson Hotel had become rundown and dilapidated near the end, catering mainly to transients. The Jefferson had fifty-eight hotel rooms that could be rented by the night, week or month. Monthly rent cost as little as $250 a month as of 1990. "We acquired it at around the time we got the Hotel LaSalle and moved forward to relocate everyone," Hammond mayor Thomas McDermott Jr. told *The Times of Northwest Indiana*. "We can't develop a business district if there are all these transients downtown. We got a lot of complaints from the business community about people standing around and just standing in front of buildings. It's not conducive to the business environment we're trying to create."

THE LYNDORA HOTEL

The long-defunct Lyndora Hotel, which Pullman-Standard built by its plant on Hammond's east side for visiting management, once hosted famed aviator Amelia Earhart, who addressed the Hammond Junior Women's Club at Hammond High School. "Amelia's appearance in the city was quite the talk of the town," according the Hammond Historical Society newsletter. "On the next day, the social column of the daily newspaper was abuzz by her visit." More than nine hundred turned out to hear Earhart, who revealed she relied on tomato juice to sustain her nutritionally during her long flights. "It was reported that Amelia Earhart had conquered Hammond that evening with the ease that she flew over the Atlantic and Pacific Oceans," the Hammond Historical Society said in its *Flashback* newsletter. "Her gracious personality and keen sense of humor captured the hearts of the near capacity audience at the high school auditorium. That night, she asked the question, 'how many of you would go up in a modern plane if I were at the controls?' All but a half dozen quickly raised their hands up high."

She talked about her preparations for her upcoming flight across the Pacific Ocean, with many humorous asides. "Miss Earhart said she liked to fly for the beauty of the view over both the land and sea," reported the *Flashback*. "She had no plans for any future flight but may develop an idea overnight for another attempt at time and distance. Of her journeys, she stated that her chances for success over the Atlantic were 1 in 10 against her, whereas the odds against her on the Pacific flight were about 50-50."

HOHMAN HOUSE

Another of downtown Hammond's grand hotels, the seven-story, $500,000 Hohman House Hotel Building at Clinton Street and Hohman Avenue went up in the 1920s with Gothic, brick and terra-cotta stylings as a sister property to the Southmoor Hotel Apartments. The hotel boasted 164 rooms it rented out for two to three dollars a night. Fully equipped with amenities, the Hohman House boasted two elevators, a restaurant, a writing room, lounges and an elegantly designed lobby. Also long gone, the Majestic Hotel and Cafe at Hohman Avenue and State Street promised visitors a lot on its storefront signs: "steaks, chops, fish, oysters, Pabst Blue Ribbon beer, billiards, cigars, tobacco, smokers supplies" and even "tables for ladies."

HOWARD JOHNSON'S/RAMADA INN

As Hammond suburbanized, hotels shifted from downtown to by the highways. The iconic American chain Howard Johnson's came to Hammond early in its rapid national expansion of motor lodge and restaurant complexes. In 1959, the iconic American chain opened a location at 4135 Calumet Avenue just south of the Indiana Toll Road serving Hammond and Chicago's Southeast Side. In 1963, it offered all-you-can-eat fried chicken with french fries, coleslaw and rolls with butter. Children under twelve could enjoy the same meal for just $0.98. In 1960, one could buy a clam and flounder feast for just $1.99. HoJo was the largest restaurant chain in the United States in the 1960s and 1970s, but times and tastes change. In the 2000s, the Hammond location was turned into a Johnel's Restaurant and Lounge, a Ramada Inn, a Super Inn Motel and Dynasty Banquets, which remains a popular destination for weddings, gatherings and Lakeshore Chamber of Commerce get-togethers. There's a small Statue of Liberty replica outside a restaurant where one can grab omelets, bacon and eggs or other hearty Greek diner fare.

11
RESTAURANTS

PHIL SMIDT'S

The lake perch and frog leg palace Phil Smidt's was known from far and wide, lasting nearly a century. Phil Smidt's at 1205 Calumet Avenue near the lakefront made it just shy of a century before closing for good in 2007 in what some patrons compared to the death of a family member. The fifteen-thousand-square-foot seafood restaurant that could seat up to 450 diners served hundreds of millions of plates of fried fish and frog legs and cups of its original chowder to generations of Hammond residents in what a Yelp reviewer called "family-style dining at its best" and another online reviewer said had the "best lake perch on the planet." Frank Sinatra dined there. So did Bob Hope and many other famous people. So did countless travelers along U.S. 12, U.S. 20 and U.S. 41 despite the pungent soap smells from the neighboring Lever Brothers soap factory. "If you were a frog between 1910 and 2007, you would have wanted to stay away from Whiting," according to *The Times of Northwest Indiana*. "Phil Smidt's Restaurant became known as the place to go for frog legs, although it originally was billed as a fish and chicken restaurant. The restaurant operated for 97 years, in the soap-scented shadow of the Unilever plant." Originally an ice cutter at Wolf Lake, Smidt ran one of the establishments Hammond historically has been best known for, but the restaurant only ended up in the city by chance. "Phil Smidt got off a train in Hammond because he needed a pair of shoes," F. Derril Reed wrote in the Hammond's Historical Society's *Pages from the Past*. "He worked to get the money for them and then was refused his pay,

Phil Smidt's burned down in 1945. *Hammond Public Library.*

although they gave him the shoes. He rose rapidly in the ice-cutting industry to the superintendency of what amounted to a year-round job and thus he stayed for 25 years—until 1910, when he quit and started in the restaurant business." He would sometimes work until 2:00 a.m. supervising icehouses, fixing machinery, caring for the horses or cutting hay in the summer for the straw that kept the icehouses insulated at the time.

"The cutting was done by men operating saws pulled by horses." Reed wrote. "It was hazardous-some men would slip under the ice and were never seen again." They would cut ice from December through mid-March, when it was bitterly cold that close to the inland ocean of Lake Michigan, which remains notorious for its lake-effect wind chill to this day. They sent up to 150 freight cars a day up to the packinghouses in Chicago. "Many of the laborers were itinerant and would show up with straw hats," Reed wrote. "Then later they were noted wearing shawls around their heads and with newspapers tied around their shoes."

Phil Smidt's built up an excellent reputation based on the quality of the food and its coast-to-coast advertising. In the 1940s and 1950s, cars lined up

The Phil Smidt's perch palace was a big draw to Hammond. *Hammond Public Library.*

for blocks for a hot plate of comfort food at the legendary institution, which was a lily pad–length hop from the Illinois border on Chicago's far South Side. It was where Hammond residents took out-of-town relatives who were visiting. It was allegedly even at one point a haunt for the Chicago Outfit, whose leaders migrated from the south suburbs farther and farther into Northwest Indiana to evade attention from authorities. *Chicago Tribune* food writer Majorie David said the restaurant—which is in a highly industrialized area by a sometimes foul-smelling Cargill processing plant—"was close to Lake Michigan, but not in a scenic spot" in a "three out of four forks" review that questioned the prevailing wisdom that frog legs taste like chicken. "It's better, more delicate and the texture is lighter, almost flaky," she wrote, while dismissing the list of largely by-the-glass wines as "pedestrian."

The vino may have been modest because Phil Smidt's started out as a clapboard roadhouse before it had to be rebuilt. An explosion rocked the longtime Hammond restaurant on January 29, 1945.

"When the fire department first arrived, there was no fire—only cement dust that was falling like a fine mist," Gordon D. Whitney wrote in the

Hammond Historical Society's *History of the Hammond, Indiana Fire Department*. He continued,

> *Parts of the walls were standing and the roof had fallen in on one side, giving the appearance of a house of cards. A gas leak has brought on the explosion. Climbing through the wreckage, the fireman began to sift through the ruins, looking for bodies. The blue light from the ruptured gas line continued to burn. Some time had passed when the ground shook and flames could be seen shooting up eight feet along the fence in front of Lever Brothers. Evidently, the gas had traveled underneath Indianapolis Boulevard. The searching went on and the temperature began to drop soon, going to below zero.*

NIPSCO tried to reroute the lines, but it was too late. Firefighters were forced to try to stop the blaze from spreading to surrounding buildings. But it was not routine fire. "It wasn't long before the cold night was filled with exploding shotgun shells caused from the heat of the fire," Whitney wrote.

A fire forced Phil Smidt's to rebuild. *Hammond Public Library.*

"'Pete' Smidt kept a large supply of ammunition in his personal apartment. The men had a double job of fighting a fire and dodging shotgun pellets." Four died in the tragic fire. "It was a good thing that the fire happened when it did for if it happened two hours later, the place would have been filled with the dinner crowd," Whitney wrote.

Phil Smidt's put Hammond on the map, reeling in travelers on nearby train tracks and who took U.S. 12, U.S. 20 and U.S. 41, including many vacation-bound Chicagoans. It was an experience, with several dining rooms, a bar, a powder room and walls lined with old news clippings, memorabilia and plenty of lake perch and frog legs iconography. It enthusiastically embraced kitsch, at one point selling a T-shirt with frog legs line-dancing like Rockettes and high-kicking while wearing tuxedos and top hats. Founded in 1910, Phil Smidt's served 35,000 pairs of frog legs and 12,000 gallons of tartar sauce a month during its prime, according to *Lost Recipes Found.* Workers at local steel mills in Northwest Indiana and South Chicago often lunched there, but it also drew visitors from across the Midwest on the strength of its well-known reputation. The restaurant estimates it sold 135 to 140 tons of lake perch each year and another 70,000 tons of frog legs, which were then and remain today more of an acquired taste. "Phil Smidt's has been a gathering place for wedding receptions, anniversaries, showers, proms and funeral luncheons for 97 years," owner David Welch told *The Times of Northwest Indiana* when it closed in 2007. After filing for bankruptcy in 2003, Phil Smidt's shuttered a few years later, laying off sixty employees, according to *The Times*. The city has since bought and demolished the building. The owners talked about bringing it back at a new location, possibly on U.S. 30 near the Southlake Mall, closer to where much of the population in Lake County shifted, but those plans never materialized and longtime diners have been left to seek recommendations for replacements like Teibel's and to share recipes online for the cornmeal-coated perch, coleslaw, frog legs and bean salad. The restaurant staked its reputation on Region delicacies that were once fished from Lake Michigan and drenched in melted butter, with more butter on the side. The perch was pan-fried and either boned or whole, head and all, served with ramekins of parsley-flecked tartar sauce for dipping, and the fall-off-the-bone frog legs were either sautéed or deep-fried. One could order an all-you-can-eat portion, and many did. "This is a family type of restaurant. The menu isn't fancy. It doesn't have a sous chef," Welch told *The Times*. "This is basic home food. It had two items on the menu that did 70 percent of the business, frog legs and perch. We were known for it. Frogs were used a lot in the advertisements because you could play with frogs, like clowns."

No one ever left hungry, with bounteous bread baskets and relish trays with beets, kidney beans, coleslaw, potato salad and cottage cheese reputedly from a Porter County farm. It offered many desserts, including bread pudding and pie that could be served à la mode. It was a resolutely old-school place, with décor unchanged from the 1950s, where one could find a gooseberry pie long after it fell out of fashion.

The place had a sense of humor, such as with the "Standard Oil Special" dessert on the menu. The pound cake accompanied by ice cream and doused in three different colored syrups was meant to look like an oil spill. Beyond the lake perch and frog legs it was famous for, entrées included walleye, pike, smoked whitefish, catfish, salmon, shrimp, lobster tail and Alaskan snow crab. Prices ranged from the affordable for local factory workers to the more upscale.

Phil Smidt's suffered many setbacks over the years, including the addition of the Borman Expressway, the Indiana Toll Road, the Horseshoe Casino and the construction of an overpass from Indianapolis Boulevard to the

A bystander watched Phil Smidt's burn in 1945. *Hammond Public Library.*

A fire laid waste to Phil Smidt's, the restaurants known for its lake perch and frog legs. *Hammond Public Library.*

gambling boat in 1995 that diverted much of the traffic away. Once on the main highway through Northwest Indiana, it ended up geographically isolated in an area hard-hit by demographic changes that meant less disposable income in the immediate vicinity. After shunning the eatery for years, diners flocked back for one last taste of the famous lake perch and frog legs, waiting as long as three hours for a table before it closed. "I was afraid they were going to run out of perch but they didn't. It was lovely. I've been coming since I moved and my husband, who worked at Sinclair, brought me here; I come in memory of him," Calumet City resident Wilma Fisher told *The Times* in 2007. "We had the kids' graduation parties here. It's a wonderful place, and I hate to see it go." Some online reviewers complained about the declining quality, cheaper ingredients and poor management over the years, dismissing perch as "scrawny" and "a shadow of its former self," according to a LTH Forum discussion online that said Phil Smidt's is "beyond criticism" and "not all about the food." The long-vacant Phil Smidt's building was razed in 2015 with little fanfare.

VOGEL'S RESTAURANT

Vogel's Restaurant closed seventy-seven years after Fred and Iga Vogel opened it on Calumet Avenue in 1921, displacing about twenty-five workers. It was one of the Region's top dining spots, a supper club–like institution that served lake perch, frog and its signature Shrimp de Jonghe. It was considered a "fancy" eatery that often hosted wedding receptions, banquets and parties, according to *The Times of Northwest Indiana*. "Some called it a restaurant but I say it was a roadhouse because why else did all these big limousines come out from Chicago," Maurey Zlotnik wrote in the Hammond Historical Society's *Pages from the Past*. "At the end of every football season for four years, (Fred Vogel) would give a party for the team, all the coaches and all, and I tell you we had all the fish, chicken and fries we could eat."

The 850-seat restaurant that settled at 1250 Indianapolis Boulevard in Hammond in 1944 established itself as a local landmark that served lake perch to many businesspeople with expense accounts who had business with local factories. Fred Vogel's son Bob Vogel, a high school football star, took over, but the once-bustling restaurant eventually faded. "The factories have moved out," owner Janis Vogel Hahn told *The Times of Northwest Indiana*. "The laws as to drinking and expense accounts have changed. A lot of the businesses left in the area have had to cut costs. We can't get lake perch and it's too expensive. But the riverboats are what finally made us realize we couldn't go on." The casino sucked up all the traffic to the area around Vogel's. "Once they opened their delis, dining and banquet rooms that charge such reasonable prices, we knew we couldn't compete," Hahn said. "And when people come on buses, they don't stop at the local restaurants." She said there was a possibility it could reopen, but bigger old-school restaurants were largely no longer viable because of taxes, overhead and insurance.

MINER-DUNN

Miner-Dunn Real Hamburgers and Schoop's are perhaps the two purest versions of the Region-style burger, the meaty, griddle-edged burger built for the working man. It's long been camped on Indianapolis Boulevard in Highland but got its start in Hammond in 1932. Harold Miner and Ralph Dunn started the restaurant with eighty dollars and "one heck of a hamburger" at 5440 Calumet Avenue in a small space with just six stools.

Miner-Dunn first opened in Hammond. *Photo by author.*

"When Hammond's Civic Center came on board in 1938, all the little restaurants on Calumet Avenue and nearby benefited. I can still remember how we looked forward to a stop at Miner-Dunn, which sold, in my opinion, the best hamburger in the Calumet Region," Region historian and *The Times of Northwest Indiana* columnist Archibald McKinlay wrote. "Others will argue that the best hamburger came from Made-Rite. Technically, that wasn't a hamburger at all. Made-Rite burgers featured all loose ingredients, and had a few extras thrown in for good measure." Miner-Dunn opened multiple locations across Northwest Indiana and south suburban Chicago in Illinois, but only the Highland spot remains, though its parking lot is usually packed in the evenings. Rival Schoops, which now has nearly twenty locations across Northwest Indiana and the south suburbs, also got its start in Hammond in 1948 and remains in the city to this day with a location at 7235 Indianapolis Boulevard—you can still get a bottomless coffee with your chili in a throwback environment.

BREAD BASKET

The once popular Bread Basket at 7205 Indianapolis Boulevard in Hammond's Woodmar neighborhood served its last loaf in 2015, after nearly three decades. "Sometimes when it's done, it's done," owner Ron Lineburg told *The Times*. "This is closed. We're just looking to see what the next step is." Ron and Karen Lineburg ground their own grain to bake fresh bread every day since the restaurant opened in 1986 as a way to pay his tuition at the Moody Bible Institute in Chicago. Bread Basket started out on Calumet Avenue but proved so popular as to be able to move to a much larger, two-story space on Indianapolis Boulevard. The eatery, a favorite with professors and students at the nearby Purdue University–Calumet, now Purdue University–Northwest in Hammond, served up soup, salads and sandwiches, including the top-selling almond chicken sandwich, tuna salad sandwich, onion casserole and baked potato soup. The half sandwich–half soup combos were especially popular at the resolutely retro eatery that was adorned with woven baskets and other casual country décor. Efforts to modernize with contemporary fare like paninis, seasonal menus and vegetarian options failed, as did other long-established restaurants in the Region that called it quits around the same time, including Bronko's in Crown Point, the Patio in Merrillville, Strongbow Inn in Valparaiso and Rodini's in Michigan City.

BLUE ROOM CAFE

The Blue Room Cafe was relatively short-lived in downtown Hammond after relocating from Highland. It was at one point during the early 2000s one of the three coffee shops to occupy Hammond's south suburb of Highland. The owner moved north to 5246 Hohman Avenue in the heart of downtown Hammond when the opportunity presented itself. A cozy space filled with the work of local artists that was popular with downtown Hammond attorneys, the funky eclectic café established an annual Beatles Fest that outlived it and grew into a massive outdoor festival that draws hundreds downtown every summer for cover bands playing Beatles songs. The Blue Room Cafe occupied a prominent, highly visible spot but kept limited hours since downtown Hammond catered mainly to office workers—though one could often find poets, songwriters or other creative types scribbling in notebooks there. It was replaced by the Stella Vita Cafe, founded by a former 18th Street Brewery brewer who was taking classes at the Hammond Development Center across the street, which relocated after a few years into the Northern District of Indiana federal courthouse down the street, where most of its customers resided. It's far from the only coffee shop in Hammond, which has long been home to many Dunkin' Donuts and has since added two Starbucks since the Blue Room Cafe stopped percolating its own potent brew.

12

TRAINS

Trains have long bedeviled Hammond residents since neighboring Chicago is one of the biggest railroad hubs in the nation, being in the middle of the country and near the south shore of Lake Michigan under which cross-country trains must pass. The railroads were largely responsible for driving Hammond's early growth. As Hammond librarian Carol Williams wrote in *A Brief History of the Hammond Public Library*,

> *While trains may be an inconvenience today as we go about our daily routines, railroads in the late 1800s were predominant and a main reason why the Region grew so quickly. From the counting of the first US Census in 1880 to 1900, Hammond's population grew from 699 to 12,376—a 1,670 percent increase in twenty years. It was a hub of commercial activity as goods crossed the country. Passenger trains connecting local towns and running through downtown Hammond, quickly made Hammond the shopping center of Lake County. And when service from Hammond to Chicago at 63rd Street began, it made Hammond even more of an ideal spot for businesses looking for new locations. Big business found Hammond especially appealing because the land available for expansion and the easy access to both the rail lines and the Grand Calumet River as transportation avenues, would allow them to prosper.*

But the trains were a double-edged sword. While they brought people, commerce, bustle and industry, they made it hard to get around Hammond from nearly the start. Hammond residents have often found themselves stuck at intersections waiting on freight trains, oil cars and the South Shore Line. But the train mess was even more pronounced in the city's early days when trains were more prevalent and regulations more lax. "No memories of Hammond in the 1920s would be complete without recalling how Hammond was tied up by trains in those days," O'Hern wrote in the Hammond Historical Society's *Pages from the Past*.

> *The Erie was the major culprit. It was helped significantly by the Nickel Plate, the Monon, the New York Central, the Wabash, and Hammond's very own Indiana Harbor Belt. The Erie in particular specialized in switching when the town was crowded by shoppers—or so it seemed. Hohman, State, Sibley and all the side streets would be jammed with halted traffic. Horns would be blowing. And all the while the freight cars just stood there. After ten or fifteen minutes the train would move a car length ahead, and then come to a stop again. Then after another five or ten minutes the train would back up half a car length. And so on—and on—and on.*

The inconvenience of the trains is credited with diverting business away from downtown. *The Times* estimated that five thousand railroad boxcars passed through the city every day and delayed drivers at more than one hundred rail street crossings. Residents were forced to wait for trains half the time at the busy corner of State and Hohman in the heart of downtown. "What killed downtown Hammond was the railroads," longtime Hammond councilman-at-large George Carlson told *The Times*.

13

STANDARD STEEL CAR COMPANY/ PULLMAN-STANDARD FACTORY

The real estate firm of William Gostlin, Peter W. Meyn and A. Murray Turner partnered with *Lake County Times* publisher Sidmon McHie to convince Standard Steel Car Company executive James B. "Diamond Jim" Brady to bring railroad freight car manufacturing to the city. Overnight, Standard Steel Car became Hammond's largest employer with 3,500 workers in 1912. It employed up to 5,000 workers until the 1930s, when it was sold to industrialist George Pullman's Pullman Company, becoming the Standard-Pullman Car Manufacturing Company and ultimately producing hundreds of thousands of freight and passenger railroad cars. The factory that produced cattle cars, flat cars, bag cars, express cars, and steel passenger cars was believed to have boosted the fledgling city's population by about 12,000. "Hammond's economy was closely linked to its payroll," according to the *Hammond, Indiana American Bicentennial Yearbook*. "It was located on the far southeastern section of Hammond in 1906 and the area known as East Hammond sprang up with housing for its employees almost at once. The streetcar company extended its tracks down Conkey Street to a point just one block from the main entrance."

Executives and workers of the factory lived in a highly ethnic East Hammond subdivision that since has become known as the Standard Pullman Historic Community; it was home to Germans, Hungarians, Slovaks, Romanians, Bulgarians, Lithuanians, Russians, Greeks, Italians, Croatians, Polish, Armenians and Swiss, according to the Hammond Historical Society.

Standard Steel Car was one of Hammond's largest employers during the early nineteenth century and was the site of a major strike. *Hammond Public Library.*

The company also built the plush Lyndora Hotel for visiting company management during 1918. Facing Maywood Park, it charged $1.50 per room and $3.00 for a room with a bath. Named after the president's daughter, it offered excellent fine dining and was so elegant it was featured on postcards. The hotel was later transformed into senior citizen housing.

The Standard Steel Car factory, which cut wages by 40 to 60 percent and docked rent from payroll checks, was a site of much labor strife in those early days. "Numerous labor problems of the Standard Steel Rail Car Co. led to the strike movement and the altercation on Sept. 9, 1919—killing four workers and injuring over 60 people," the Hammond Historical Society said in its *Flashback* newsletter. "This news headline became known as the 'Hammond Massacre.'" Several hundred workers left their jobs months before the strike after the company refused to meet with the American Federation of Labor Unions at a time when iron- and steel workers were unionizing across Chicagoland, but labor leader Samuel Gompers brokered a deal for them to return to work. But the company insisted it could not afford raises. Indiana governor J.P. Goodrich threatened to impose martial law on the city as troops were deployed to quell potential riots. "Tempers were roused and numerous arrests were made," according to the Hammond Historical Society. Workers demanded an immediate pay raise of 10 percent, another pay raise of 10 percent within sixty days, no rents charged for unoccupied company houses, recognition for a grievance committee and an end to bribing foremen to land a job. As may as two thousand men thronged the streets, reportedly hitting police officers with bricks and hoses. Crowds, including workers armed with clubs and blackjacks, sought to prevent anyone from entering the plant. They tossed stones and other projectiles at any vehicles trying to enter the plant, including the chauffeured car plant manager G.H. Vincent tried to enter with, according to Hammond Historical Society's Joseph Piekarczyk. "Everything moveable—benches, barrels, kegs, boards, railroad ties, smaller timbers, and garbage cans—seemed to be thrown into the street and at the machine in an effort to stop it," Piekarczyk wrote in *The Standard Steel Car Strike of 1919*. "The board of the car was dented, the windshield shattered and the top ripped open, but fortunately few of the missiles struck the occupants." The police later opened fire on a crowd of more than five hundred strikers, killing Steven Krawczek, George Rosko, Stanley Skies and Lawrence Dudek. Both sides claimed the other

A Pullman worker operates a lathe while building a railcar in Hammond. *Hammond Public Library.*

Hammond has made railroad cars and many other products over the years. *Hammond Public Library.*

fired the first shot. *The Times* headlines screamed "Fierce Riots at Standard Steel" and "Fights and Brawls on Every Hand—Shots Fill the Air, Almost Everybody This Morning Bears Evidence of Fray." The strike did not get resolved until a Lake County judge and the city intervened. Many workers had since sought employment elsewhere or returned to Europe. It was one of "the most violent strikes in Region history at the time but almost unnoticed at the national level."

The train car giant Pullman, known for its own labor relations woes and impeccably dapper Pullman porters, bought out Standard Steel Car Company in 1929 and merged Pullman Car & Manufacturing with it in 1934. Following the acquisition, workers built railroad cars at the Pullman-Standard factory at 165th Street and Columbia Avenue. Pullman bused them in, and they also took the train to work and walked from the nearby eastside neighborhood the company built for its employees in Hammond, which was initially filled with tenement housing that was eventually eradicated by the city's slum-clearance program. Later, the

Pullman neighborhood was all single-family homes with façades of stone, brick, stucco and shingles after the company slapped up "180 houses in 90 days," according to *The Times*. During World War II, the plant was pressed into military service and enlisted to make M-4 Sherman Tanks with 7mm cannons in revolving turrets. The hulking tanks lined 165th Street as a source of patriotic pride as the Pullman-Standard plant supplied the Allies on the front lines, scratching off the production numbers on the side before loading them on railcars so enemy spies couldn't deduce how many were being made, an article on the *Hammond High School Class of 1959* webpage stated: "It provided high-paying jobs for the Region and a great deal of patriotic pride in addition to winning the war." There was also a research component that employed many white-collar professionals. "The largest laboratory for the testing of railroad cars in the world is located in the present-day plant of the Pullman-Standard Company on Fields Street, just east of Columbia Avenue," according to the *Hammond, Indiana American Bicentennial Yearbook*. "Processes of control and new development have come quietly out of this new division of the old Pullman Company in spite of the moribund state in which old railroads find themselves as to their finances. It is in these laboratory research areas that the solution to this all-necessary form of transportation will eventually be found." After more than seven decades of rail car production, the factory closed its doors for good in 1982.

14

TAYLOR CHAIN COMPANY

S.G. Taylor Jr. established the Taylor Chain Company factory in Hammond by combining his father's Chicago firm with the U.S. Chain Company in Indiana. The company's chains were used by the thriving local steel industry, railroads, lake boat companies and the agricultural industry. "Each coil is cut by a cutting machine into links known as 'scarf links' which are then heated by ovens fired in oil," according to the *Calumet Region Historical Guide*. "On becoming white-hot they are pounded into shape by hand and then an arm hammer. Larger links are formed from a foot-long straight pin which, because coke causes a hotter fire than oil, has been heated in a coke oven. Every chain, made of the links that are formed, is tested for durability by placing each end in an iron arm and pulling. After this test, it is inspected for defective links." Cornell University graduate Edward Winthrop Taylor took over the family business in 1936, when he was the first in the industry to introduce flash welding of alloy steels, which strengthened the company's reputation.

The company survived the Great Depression by employing workers for six months, laying them off for another six months and replacing them with "another old hand." During World War II, it swelled to 350 workers and was the first in the Calumet Region to earn the coveted E award. The chain manufacturer grew from 20,000 square feet in Hammond to 150,000 square feet in 1961 and added a second plant in Pittsburgh. Its Hammond plant at the Illinois State Line and 141st Street near the state line on the city's north side went from 11 employees at first to more than 300 in the early

1970s, serving both consumers and local steel mills. "This firm had been through two World Wars and has been cited for high-quality production and forward vision in the improvement of the chain-making process by the U.S. government so that now their quality products of a dizzying variety of chains encompass the globe," according to *The Hammond, Indiana Bicentennial Yearbook.* "This is an exceptional example of the type of industry that has grown with Hammond and shared its ups and downs." The factory produced hundreds of different chains, including some that were seldom used.

Unionized in 1967, Taylor Chain Company eventually shuttered in the early 1980s after protracted seven-week strike that was immortalized in by Kartemquin Films' *Taylor Chain I* & *II* documentary films. The movies were acclaimed for a gritty depiction of blue-collar life, following workers from the factory floor to the union hall to the picket line as they sought higher wages and better working conditions in the early 1970s. The workers hoped to be paid $4.70 an hour, or more than $25.00 an hour in today's dollars.

The recipients of the William Friedkin Award at the Chicago International Film Festival and the International Labor Communications Association Film & Broadcast Award, the films directed by Jerry Blumenthal and Gordon Quinn were broadcast on public television. It was one of the few documentary films to focus on the process of collective bargaining. "Unions are one of the last bastions of democracy that have a direct and legitimate effect on people's lives," Blumenthal told *The Times of Northwest Indiana.* The second installment depicts how union and management negotiated at a Holiday Inn conference room to try to save the plant from recession and the effects of globalization, which they ultimately fail to do despite striking an agreement.

A shell of its former self with a drastically reduced workforce, the company closed for good in 1983 after filing for bankruptcy. Taylor Chain Company's legacy was cyanide contamination; it used the chemical to treat steel for fencing, according to the *Hammond, Indiana American Bicentennial Yearbook.* STA Decanting had to clean up the site after buying Taylor's former plant in the mid-1980s, according to *The Times of Northwest Indiana* archives.

15
W.B. CONKEY/RAND McNALLY PLANT

W.B. Conkey and later Rand McNally once made maps, travel guides and countless books at a plant at 649 Conkey Street in Hammond. It sprang up just as the G.H. Hammond meatpacking plant burned down, sustaining a city that could have been crippled economically. The W.B. Conkey Company was founded in Chicago in 1877 and constructed a grand bookbinding plant at 617 Conkey Street in Hammond twenty years later that was sold to Rand McNally in 1949. Conkey moved his fast-growing operation out of the Loop in search of search of a new labor market. Architect George Newman designed the building, which was noteworthy for allowing natural light in through the sawtooth roof. Construction was finished in under a year, and the new plant opened on the Fourth of July in 1898. "Great joy came to the city in 1898 when the Conkey Book Bindery came and gave occupations to many workers, especially to those young women who had had only domestic work in Chicago," Maria Hesterman wrote in the Hammond Historical Society's *Pages from the Past*. "Factories in those days started at 7 a.m. and closed at 6 p.m. The wages were from two to three dollars per week for a six-day week. The book bindery was a great help to many Hammond families all with very small cash incomes and Conkey Street then came into existence. There were no homes built south of this street. All was wooded area."

Company literature described the book manufacturing factory as a "mammoth printing and binding works." "It was then considered the largest book-binding operation in the world and the new building, with

Opposite, top: The W.B. Conkey Plant was a major Hammond employer. *Hammond Public Library.*

Opposite, bottom: Workers at the W.B. Conkey Plant in Hammond bound books for decades. *Hammond Public Library.*

Above: The W.B. Conkey Plant in Hammond produced Bibles, novels and many other books. *Hammond Public Library.*

its famous sawtooth roof, became a source of new pride in Hammond at once," according to the *Hammond, Indiana American Bicentennial Yearbook*. "Mr. Conkey paid for his streetcar tracks to be extended to his plant eastward from Hohman Avenue." Initially, the factory was powered by steam. Much of the work was done by hand, including dipping the marble edges of Webster's Dictionary and the gold edges of Bibles by hand. It printed collections of poetry, the Sears-Roebuckc catalogue, the *Conkey Home Magazine* and William Jennings Bryan's "Cross of Gold" speech. The W.B. Conkey Printing and Publishing Establishment employed 1,100 and generated $3 million a year around 1900. The print works received commissions from many prominent clients, such as Armour & Company, International Harvester, Standard Oil and the Fair Store. "It is claimed that there is not another equal to it in the United States or in Europe; and one who goes through the different rooms, sees the machinery at work, and looks at what is accomplished by human skill, may quite readily accept that statement," historian T.H. Ball wrote in *Northwestern Indiana From 1800 to 1900: A View of our Region through the Nineteenth Century*. "Hammond was just the place for such an immense industry, where room for buildings was abundant and where there would be no need for a second of third story, not suggesting a fourteenth." Ball toured the sweeping plant, which covered an area of up to twenty acres and housed forty-two presses in room that ran "hundreds of feet in their dimension." He was wowed:

> *The folding and binding room is long and wide and high, with plenty of light from the sunlight whiteout, and while the well-trained and nimble fingers of the girls who fold by hand accomplish rapid work and show what trained human hands and eyes can do in acquiring a peculiar tact of manipulation, the amazing if not fascinating features in the room are fixtures, the great folding machines, working as by clock work, folding up, hour after hour, the great sheets of sixteen pages, with the regularity of the movement of a finished chronometer. The invention of a self-binder for farming work was a great triumph of human ingenuity, but one may well stand amazed in looking upon the movements of a great folding machine.*

A great driving wheel powered many machines, like the typesetters, binders and gilders. The publishing plant turned out encyclopedias, magazines, *Reader's Digests*, dictionaries, atlases, phone books, textbooks, Great Ideas Yearbooks and Book of the Month Club publications. Ball continued:

> *A natural question would be, where can sufficient copy be found to keep the typesetters busy, so as to keep forty presses running on one room, and to keep all those girls and folding machines and gilders and binders busy month after month in the binding room? And the answer is, it comes from all quarters, comes from everywhere. Books of various kinds and printed and published, among them the American Encyclopedia, dictionaries, storybooks for children, catalogues and many varieties of printed matter.*

W.B. Conkey was one of the largest bookmaking industries in the world. In its heyday, W.B. Conkey Company was home to fifty presses, both color and black and white, "all flat-bed Miehle cylinders and high-speed verticals. The factory could produce 80,000 hardbound books per day and 200,000 paperbacks." The seven hundred workers there, some of whom accumulated

Above: The W.B. Conkey Plant in Hammond long manufactured books, pamphlets, publications and other reading materials. *Hammond Public Library.*

Left: W.B. Conkey marketed directly to consumers through the *Conkey's Home Journal*. *Hammond Public Library.*

as much as four decades of experience, also hand-bound special orders for Bibles. "Many of America's foremost publishers are among the clientele buildup during the past 60 years," according to *The Calumet Region Historical Guide*. "For the edition publishers, they make schoolbooks of many types for various publishers, book of fiction, directories, Bibles, law books, and juvenile books, all produced annually. The catalog field is equally varied, much of the output being distributed directly from Hammond."

Founder W.B. Conkey died in 1923, bequeathing the business to his son Henry. Henry Conkey was quick-witted, winning an account from the Church of Jesus Christ of Latter-day Saints on printing its Mormon Bible by suggesting the dimensions be reduced so it could fit into a coat pocket. Henry steered the business through the Great Depression, and jigsaw puzzles and Shirley Temple picture books became the biggest sources of income. The plant contributed to the war effort during World War II, printing manuals for the military. Conkey sold the business to Rand McNally, century-plus-old business with an international reach, in 1948 but stayed on until he died in 1953. By then, the factory was running

The W.B. Conkey Plant employed generations of Hammond residents. *Hammond Public Library.*

Above: Books were bound by hand at the W.B. Conkey Plant in Hammond. *Hammond Public Library.*

Left: W.B. Conkey books were staples of many living rooms, as evidenced in this vintage advertisement. *Hammond Public Library.*

The office at the W.B. Conkey Plant in Hammond. *Hammond Public Library.*

The W.B. Conkey Plant in Hammond went through a lot of paper. *Hammond Public Library.*

around the clock, printing 300,000 to 400,000 books per day, or 75 million to 100 million per year. Members of the Hammond Historical Society who toured the plant were "all awed by the incredible speed of the huge machines," according to *Tales from the Past*. The massive plants generated five to six boxcars full of wastepaper per day.

After supplying the nation with reading material for most of the twentieth century, the Rand McNally plant in Hammond closed for good in 1981 during a rough period when many factories in the city shuttered. In 1996, Hammond city officials decided to demolish part of plant to make way for a $1.1 million recycling center.

16
SEARS ROEBUCK/ALVAH ROEBUCK

Sears filed for bankruptcy in 2018, making the potential end of the store that grew into the nation's largest retailer for more than a century and that built the world's tallest skyscraper in the 1970s just because it could. The Hoffman Estates, Illinois–based retailer long ago entered a period of decline, losing ground to Target, Walmart and Amazon and losing $11 billion since 2010, the last year it turned an annual profit. Amid the so-called retailpocalypse in which the rise of e-commerce caused the fall of many traditional brick-and-mortar stores, Sears pursued Chapter 11 bankruptcy that would allow it to restructure after closing 182 underperforming Sears and Kmart stores around the country, including the Big Kmart in Griffith just south of Hammond city limits. The first Sears Roebuck catalogue was published in Hammond by the W.B. Conkey Company, one of the most modern publishing houses in America at the time. The Sears Roebuck Company was in fact named the A.C. Roebuck Company after Alvah Curtis Roebuck, a watchmaker from Hammond who responded to a newspaper ad in the *Chicago Daily News* that Minnesota businessman Richard Sears put out shortly after setting up shop on Dearborn Avenue in the Loop; Sears was seeking someone to fix watches.

The Hammond High School Class of 1959 site shares the story:

> *On March 1, 1887, he set up a shop on Dearborn Street in Chicago with a staff of three people, one to handle bookkeeping and correspondence and two stenographers. Soon after the opening of his new shop, he found a need*

A Sears Roebuck catalogue. *Hammond Public Library.*

for a watchmaker to repair watches returned by customers. On April 1, 1887, Sears ran an ad in the Chicago Daily News *which caught the eye of a young man from Hammond, Indiana. This watchmaker responded to the ad and took samples of his work to his interview with Sears, who scheduled the meetup within a few days. He was hired on the spot. This young man from Hammond was named Alvah Curtis Roebuck.*

They partnered up while both were in their twenties and launched a catalogue of watches and jewelry in 1888 that would eventually balloon to 532 pages and spawn a mail-order empire that shipped everything from furniture to snow blowers to laxatives and motor buggies, bringing the world to a still largely rural America. Region historian Archibald McKinlay wrote in his Calumet Roots column in *The Times of Northwest Indiana* that Roebuck

Sears Roebuck fonder Alvah Roebuck lived in Hammond for about fifteen years. *Hammond Public Library.*

wanted to leave his Hammond store because of romantic disappointment: "At 21, Peter (Meyn) aced out Alvah Roebuck, a Hammond watchmaker, for the hand of Magdalena Dunsing, a Lutheran pastor's daughter. Roebuck left Hammond in despair and partnered with Richard Sears in a little enterprise you may have heard of. Peter, with a partner, established a furniture store, which failed." The *Hammond, Indiana American Bicentennial Yearbook* identified Meyn as the school janitor, but the defeat and loss of his love was too much for Roebuck to bear. "Fleeing the humiliation of the event he went to Chicago and was hired by a mail order genius named Richard Sears," according to the bicentennial yearbook. "In four years from this 1886 date, the world-famous Sears and Roebuck firm was on its way, a leader amongst mercantile firms for almost a century now." He left the Region in dramatic fashion. In contemporary terms, it would be described as a mic drop. "Contrary to reports, he did not sell out," the Hammond Historical Society said in a *Flashback* newsletter. "He simply walked out carrying a small set of repair tools. Everything else was abandoned."

A Lafayette native who was unable to make a living there, Roebuck had worked as a watch repairman at a jewelry store at the corner of Hohman and

Sibley right in the heart of downtown Hammond. He moved to Hammond when he was twelve and spent about fifteen years in the city. But stung with heartbreak, he decamped for neighboring Chicago as soon as his big break came suddenly and serendipitously. Renamed Sears, Roebuck and Company in 1895, the company Roebuck and Sears started grew because of low prices, a guarantee of satisfaction and a catalogue written in direct language that was easy to understand. Stressed by the demands of the business and wanting a quieter life, Roebuck sold his stock—one-third of the company's value—for just $25,000 in 1895. About a century later, the company's annual revenue would surpass $59 billion a year. According to the Entrepreneur Hall of Fame, Roebuck was asked later in life if he regretted selling his stake too soon when Sears went on to accumulate greater wealth. "He's dead," Roebuck reportedly replied. "Me, I never felt better." He returned to the company twice, once to run a department that sold watches, jewelry, phonographs, optical goods and eventually magic lanterns and major motion picture machines. After retiring to Florida, Roebuck suffered major financial losses during the Great Depression and was compelled to return to work in Chicago. In semiretirement, he ended up compiling a history of the company that would grow into America's largest retailer and travel around the country to Sears stores. McKinlay summarized Roebuck's roller coaster of a life aptly and succinctly in a *Times of Northwest Indiana* column in 1995:

> ROEBUCKED: *What happens when a person is thrown from a career, gets on a more successful career, is thrown again, and decides on a gentler way of life—from Alvah Roebuck who, in the late 19th century, operated a jewelry store in Hammond. When he was spurned by his lady fair, he sold his business and answered an ad in a Chicago paper for a jewelry repairman. The resulting association with the advertiser, Richard Sears, became Sears, Roebuck & Co. Not comfortable with his partner's life on the cusp of bankruptcy, Roebuck withdrew from the company and started several companies of his own, some of which produced his own inventions. When the crash wiped him out, Roebuck returned to Sears Roebuck & Company and became a roving goodwill ambassador.*

Sears of course ascended to great heights, figuratively with its presence as an anchor department store in nearly every suburban shopping mall across the country and literally with Fazlur Rahman Khan's 110-story Sears Tower, which was the tallest skyscraper in the world for twenty-five years after it was built in 1973 and remains the tallest in Chicago. Sears was

America's largest retailer until 1989, employing more than 350,000 people and spawning many successful offshoots: Craftsman, Allstate Insurance, Discover Card, Land's End, DieHard, Everlast, Joe Boxer and National Tire and Battery brands. But its profits peaked at $1.5 billion in 2006, and it lost money year over year after 2010, after failing to adapt. Sears ended up in bankruptcy court in 2018, planned to closed hundreds of more stores and face an uncertain future, with many industry observers saying its demise was only a matter of time even if it survived the bankruptcy filing. The 126-year-old retailer had 3,500 brick-and-mortar stores in 2010 but expected to emerge from bankruptcy with only 425 stores employing 45,000 people in the United States. In 2019, the troubled chain announced it would close its last remaining full-service department store in Northwest Indiana, the Sears at Southlake Mall, as it shifted focus nationally to small-format stores. One analyst said that regardless of what changes Sears made, the vaunted company had no clear path to profitability, but no one can dispute its enduring legacy or that it had a great run.

17

STRAUBE PIANO COMPANY

In 1904, the Straube Piano Company moved its manufacturing operations and executive offices from Downers Grove, Illinois, to Hammond. The piano maker took over a five-story building north of Oak Hill Cemetery, where it produced up to three thousand pianos a year. Straube cranked out the Hammond, Gilmore and Woodward lines. It took over a former blacksmith shop, shoe repair business and apartment building on Hohman Avenue downtown, where it could have an expanded showroom. On January 20, 1915, the Straube Piano Company opened in downtown Hammond with "large showrooms and a second-floor concert hall." according to the Hammond Historical Society's *Flashback* newsletter. Historian Archibald McKinlay noted Enfrid Jacobson and his brothers opened a music store in the Indiana Harbor neighborhood of East Chicago that went under because of the automatic player piano craze. But they went on to establish one of the most successful piano manufacturers in the country at a time when pianos where commonplace in middle-class living rooms. "Dear Santa Claus: I am a little girl 10 years old. I go to the Wallace School. I write you a letter but forgot to tell you my number," Clara McCoy wrote to Santa Claus in 1909, as reported by *The Times of Northwest Indiana*. "Please Santy, get the piano at Straube's. I don't care what kind it is, so you buy it there. The factory is by the Conkey Plant. I don't want everything. Give the other little children that haven't got any papas lots of nice things. Goodbye Santa."

The business at 5241 Hohman Avenue sold pianos and became the "largest music merchandise house in Northern Indiana," McKinlay wrote in his Calumet Roots archive. "Eventually, Enfrid took over the factory, which employed 250, many of them Swedes who were master carpenters, and turned out a dozen or more completed pianos a day all year long," McKinlay wrote in *The Times of Northwest Indiana*. "There was no better piano made than Straube." The business closed in 1949, as television replaced the piano as a form of entertainment in homes. The company's golden era stretched from the 1900s, when more than 360,000 pianos were sold in the United States, to the 1930s, when lifestyles were shifting, families were more likely to gather around the radio than the piano and the end of the mass-market pianos business was nigh.

The vacant former Straube Piano Factory at 252 Wildwood Road was taken over by the J.L. Metz Furniture Company in 1934. Jacob L. Metz founded the furniture maker with just $106 in capital in Chicago in 1900. It became the first furniture company to build an entire dining room and complete bedroom set under one roof. J.L. Metz Furniture Company operated out of a six-story warehouse, with each floor performing a different stage of the production process. "Work would move from floor to floor until the process was completed. Not a very efficient form of production, but it did work," the Hammond Historical Society noted in its *Flashback* newsletter. "The company initially manufactured tables and chairs. During these era furniture manufacturers were very few and far between. Most factories were small and they only specialized in one or two items, such as tables or dressers. It was up to the furniture salesmen to assemble some type of set by trying to match up pieces from different manufacturings and sell them as a set." Metz's innovation was to start manufacturing the complete sets, which required an expansion. He built a second factory in 1912 and a third in 1921 as his business grew nationally.

"The good times continued up until the 1929 economic decline that devastated the country," according to the *Flashback* newsletter. "It was at this juncture that Mr. Metz has to decide whether he wanted to continue to manufacture furniture on a grand scale or get out of the business altogether." So he decided to move to the massive 150,000-square-foot former Straube factory on a 4.5-acre site in Hammond, signing a ten-year lease on the property. After relocating from Chicago, the manufacturer hired mainly local residents, mostly women. "In fact, the Metz Furniture Company had more women employed than any other furniture company in the world by proportion," according to the *Flashback*. The company made dining room tables, chairs, cabinets and other pieces of furniture in Hammond. It was so flooded with orders it operated at near-full capacity for months after its big move.

During the Great Depression, competitors cut costs by turning to cheaper woods and veneers. But the Metz company stuck with solid birch and mahogany veneers, developing a reputation for quality that would last for decades. "The buying public noticed the great quality and craftsmanship the company put in its furniture," the Hammond Historical Society stated. "The fact that the company offered great quality at competitive pricing made its products an easy sell. One of the Metz Furniture dealers even coined the slogan 'Metz Furniture makes Cadillac quality at Buick prices.'" One of many Calumet Region factories to contribute to the war effort, the plant was repurposed to make wooden ammunition boxes for the U.S. Navy during World War II. It greatly scaled back its production of bedroom and dining room furniture and then invested in new production equipment when the war ended. Sales peaked at $3 million a year during the 1960s, when the company sold the Profile Collection of modern furniture and the Old Masters Collection, reproductions of eighteenth-century furniture. At the time, J.L. Metz Furniture Company employed three hundred, sold to dealers in Europe and made its own plywood at a sawmill in northern Michigan. Metz and later his son, Jerome L. Metz, ran a tight ship. Their company was named the cleanest and safest woodworking plant in the country by the National Association of Furniture Manufacturers. "Mr. Metz has been told by his friends that he has the only plant in the area where the floors are clean enough to eat off of," according to the *Flashback*.

The J.L. Metz Furniture Company expanded in 1966 when it bought twenty-one thousand square feet of space from the neighboring Hammond Monument Company. But the good times were short-lived. The factory closed for good in 1973. Long after it stopped housing a piano manufactory, the historic Straube building in downtown Hammond was consumed by a fire in April 2018. Hammond mayor Thomas McDermott Jr. said it was a significant loss for the downtown, especially since the city had purchased the property for $110,000 and procured a liquor license for it for another $20,000 in the hope of turning it into a restaurant or craft brewery taproom. "It's sad. We had hoped to redevelop that building and try to rebuild downtown Hammond," McDermott told *The Times of Northwest Indiana*. "Obviously, it's another blow to downtown Hammond for sure. It's a beautiful building."

18
STATE LINE GENERATING PLANT

The State Line Generating Plant on Hammond's lakefront created electricity for much of the Chicago area for more than eighty years. The coal-fired ComEd plant also was one of the top polluters in the Chicago metropolitan area, belching toxins into the atmosphere, much to the chagrin of environmental and public health groups. Studies linked such emissions to asthma, cardiac disease and early death, among other complications. Workers were exposed to mercury, coal dust and welding gases. It was one of the largest electricity-generating plants in the world, producing up to 208,000 kilowatts during the 1920s and an additional 150,000 kilowatts during the next decade.

"The State Line Generating Station, property of the Chicago District Electric Generating Corporation, sells power at wholesale to other electric distributing companies," according to *The Calumet Regional Historical Guide*. "The power is generated at 22,000 volts. This voltage is increased through the use of transformers to 33,000, 66,000 or 132,000 volts, in accordance with the requirements of distributing companies." The former Commonwealth Edison power plant was the site of the occasional disaster. An explosion—a big ball of fire that burned up all the coal dust—in 1962 killed one and injured four. Another explosion in 1998 injured seventeen workers at the plant. Firefighters had trouble putting the ensuing blaze out—because there was no power. The plant took out a full-page ad in *The Times of Northwest Indiana* to apologize and thank the firefighters for their efforts.

The State Line Generating Plant on the Hammond lakeshore, one of the worst polluters in greater Chicagoland, was eventually razed. *Hammond Public Library.*

In 2010, the U.S. Environmental Protection Agency reported the State Line Generating Plant released about 44,000 pounds of barium, copper, lead and zinc into Lake Michigan and emitted 1,180 tons of hydrochloric acid, 30,000 pounds of sulfuric acid and 143 pounds of mercury into the atmosphere. Concerns also abounded about environmental racism since about three-quarters of the nearby residents were minorities, one-fifth of whom lived below the poverty line. Its last owner, the Richmond, Virginia–based Dominion Resources, determined that new federal air quality regulations would make the 515-megawatt plant uneconomical at a time when abundant natural gas was undercutting the price and aging coal plants—forced to bid for highly competitive short-term contracts as they were shut out of more lucrative long-term deals—were shuttering around the country. About one hundred union workers lost their jobs, and the City of Hammond lost its single largest property taxpayer.

Converting it to natural gas was deemed too expensive. The boilers dated to the 1950s and 1960s. The art deco structure with intricate brickwork generated $4.5 million in property tax revenue a year. It was sorely missed, especially when it was purchased by the same principals as Beemsterboer Slag, which had stirred controversy by storing petcoke on the banks of the Calumet River in Chicago's South East Side, raising fears the lakeside site would just become another dumping ground for the petroleum byproduct—which had become far more prevalent because of the industry-wide shift to dirtier tar sands oil—which can easily become airborne and cause a number of respiratory problems. But Beemsterboer Slag's owners cleaned up the site, talking about potentially bringing in a marina for yachts and condo towers with sweeping views of the lake. But another opportunity emerged after Hammond put in bid for the widely coveted Amazon Headquarters 2, an alleged $5 billion project that would result in six-figure salaries for more than fifty thousand corporate workers. The city was one of nearly 240 in North America to try to lure the corporate headquarters. Hammond pitched the lakefront site where the State Line Generating Plant once burned coal, but the lakefront views weren't enough to entice the online retail giant, the largest retailer in the United States by volume. But it did attract the attention of data center developers, who aspired to bring a data center to the site. The Digital Crossroads project promised to bring up to $200 million in investment and 400,000 square feet of data storage to the 77-acre site, where lake breezes and water would be used to cool the warehouses full of computer servers. The redevelopment project was touted as a clean enterprise that had the potential to help transform and modernize Hammond's economy, both by hosting a start-up incubator and showing the city could be home to more high-tech ventures as well. But it came at a steep architectural cost. Save for the gate, Hammond lost most of the historic brick building designed by the architectural firm Graham, Anderson, Probst & White, whose other credits include the Civic Opera House, the Field Museum, Merchandise Mart, the Shedd Aquarium and the Wrigley Building.

19

NINE SPAN BRIDGE

It was the end of the road for the historic, seventy-fie-year-old, two-thousand-foot-long Nine Span Bridge that connected Hammond and East Chicago in 2013. The Indiana Department of Transportation demolished and, eleven months later, replaced the iconic bridge with nine distinctive steel trusses that stretched over the railroad tracks on Indianapolis Boulevard with a structure that was far less iconic. The Nine Span Bridge was the longest bridge in Indiana that did not span water. Region historian Archibald McKinlay waggishly described it as the "longest viaduct over dry land in the world" that "began to carry East Chicagoans over the Gibson Yards to fresh air." There's no denying it was a Region landmark. "For me, it always will remain in my heart as the place where one hot summer a driver who shall remain nameless crashed our yellow 1973 Oldsmobile Cutlass into a rail of the bridge during high school driver's education class," *Times of Northwest Indiana* columnist Mark Kiesling wrote. "The driver remains nameless not because I'm a nice guy, but because I've gotten too old to remember who it was. And no, it wasn't me." Chicago-based E.J. Albrecht Company started work on the landmark $750,000 bridge in 1935, which opened for traffic two years later to link two North Lake County cities that were isolated by railroad traffic. It was billed as one of the longest bridges over dry land and ultimately clocked in at seventeen spans. It was known throughout Northwest Indiana and often crossed by commuters headed to the South Shore Line train station in East Chicago, the biggest one on the route. East Chicago spokesman Steve Segura called it "an eminent landmark for the entire Region." "The bridge was a dream of local officials for 10 years prior to being built, and when finally completed, it served as a long-awaited connection between East Chicago and Hammond," Hammond Chamber of Commerce president and executive director Dave Ryan wrote in a *Times of Northwest Indiana* column in 2013. "Spanning the vast Gibson Rail Yard, the bridge and its approaches are more than 3,000 feet long. At the time of its construction, it reportedly was the longest bridge over dry land in the entire U.S. (comparable in length to Ohio River bridges such as the Market Street Bridge)."

The bridge underwent major renovation projects in 1964, 1973, 1983 and 1999, when it was shrunk from four lanes to just one in each direction; in 2005, heavy trucks were banned. It got banged up pretty badly when a semitrailer truck with a too-tall load ran through a horizontal truss connected to a vertical truss in 2003 and another semi hauling steel flats sliced through five trusses in 2004. In the end, it was mottled with brown rust and chunks of the concrete deck had fallen away. The supports deteriorated as water seeped through to bad joints, rusting the support beams. The state deemed its health "poor" in 2007, when it was one of the oldest bridges in the state. The Nine Span Bridge bore the weight of thirty thousand cars a day before becoming deemed "functionally obsolete" by INDOT. The hulking bridge was handling far more traffic than normal because of the closure of the Cline Avenue bridge earlier this year, the main link to the Inland Steel Mill, the LTV mill, the oil refineries and the casinos, making it one of the most highly trafficked highways in the Region. Designed by E.J. Albrecht Company of Chicago, the 2,100-foot-long riveted skewed Parker Truss bridge rose nearly 15 feet into the air over the Gibson Rail Yards. It was demolished by Illinois-based Dunnet Bay Construction and replaced with an $18 million bridge with concrete walls that obstructed much of the view. The new bridge, which was never given a moniker as memorable as the Nine Span Bridge or any name at all, was dedicated by local and state officials during bone-chilling winds in 2013. Its massive concrete beams were manufactured in Decatur downstate. It's still one of the busiest north–south routes in Hammond, connecting the city of East Chicago. "This is the glue that binds the two cities together," East Chicago mayor Anthony Copeland commented. He and Hammond mayor Thomas McDermott Jr. were the first to cross the new bridge, in a vintage Hudson Hornet. George Rogers and his father, John Rogers, the late owner of the long-defunct Rogers Barbeque at Indianapolis Boulevard and Ridge Road in Highland, were the first to cross the original nearly-mile-long bridge when it opened in 1937, long before it became a rusty memory.

The construction superintendent who ate breakfast at their family restaurant every morning invited them into his Ford two-door coupe for the maiden voyage. "I remember looking up at all those trusses and all that steelwork, and thinking, 'My goodness—how long is this thing?'" George Rogers told *The Times of Northwest Indiana.*

Sitting on his father's lap, he craned his head up the whole time, marveling at steel beam after steel beam splayed across the sky as they puttered by at fifteen miles per hour. He never got used to how long the bridge was. "It was a momentous occasion," he told *The Times.* He ended up a trucker who hauled slag from steel mills like Inland Steel, driving over the Nine Span Bridge with its arching steel trusses nearly every day of his working life. He felt it shake when traffic passed and always feared it would fall down like the Tacoma Narrows Bridge. "I must have crossed thousands of times, probably a million times," he told *The Times of Northwest Indiana.* "I was going down the boulevard to the mills, to the old Standard Oil and to all the different industries." When traffic passed on the other side of the bridge, Rogers could feel it shake. He always feared it was going to fall down. There was a chance the historic Nine Span Bridge could be recycled somewhere in the state. The 172.5-foot bridge spans could be repurposed elsewhere. "Its wide width for a bridge of its age as well as its massive members would make it a great candidate for reuse on a rural road, where the bridge is wide enough that it likely would meet current standards for a rural road," the Hammond Historical Society said in its *Flashback* newsletter. "It also would be useful for a non-motorized crossing, perhaps a but a trail system that is used by both cyclists and pedestrians. It would even have rooms for beaches, accommodations for people fishing from the bridge and informational kiosks. The salvaged span is a chance to preserve a small part of this beautiful historic bridge. It is a chance for someone to do what **INDOT** lacked the vision to do, which is to see the potential this span has for rehabilitation and reuse."

20
WJOB AND *THE HAMMOND TIMES*

WJOB has served as the voice of the Region for nearly a century. Though it's still going strong, it's left behind many studios across town and ended the run of many longtime programs old-timers may fondly remember. The regional radio station at 1230 AM purports to provide a "living history built on listeners." It's hosted many popular shows such as *JED in the Morning*, Steve "The Preacher" Glover's afternoon show and five different foreign-language programs, including *The Greek Hour*. "The first license issued to a radio station in the Calumet area was in 1923 and it was to Hammond-Calumet Broadcasting Corporation with Dr. George F. Courier and Lawrence J. Crowley as the licensees," owner and morning show host "JED" Jim Dedelow told *The Times*. "And even during the rough patch of bankruptcy that the previous owners had, the FCC always kept the license active." WJOB was originally located at 402 Fayette Street at Hohman Avenue but moved to 449 State Street. It was long located in a studio at 6405 Olcott Avenue across from the former Woodmar Shopping Mall, which opened in 1956 and housed the station for more than half a century. It was in one place for more than sixty years, or most of its history. The four-hundred-foot tower behind the studio off Indianapolis Boulevard reached half a million listeners in Northwest Indiana and two and a half million across the Chicago metro, Dedelow told *The Times*.

Online, it reaches listeners from thousands of miles away, including from Greece. "Best of all, we've kept the focus on listeners the same as when the station began," Dedelow told *The Times*. "We're not only on the air talking,

THAT THE PEOPLE MAY KNOW

WJOB in Hammond bills itself as "The Voice of the Region." *Hammond Public Library.*

we're also hearing what our listeners tell us. Our audience feel very close to this station, treating it as their station, and that's what we want." The station long catered to the Region's ethnic groups. "Eddie Oskierko's *Polish Musical Varieties* became one of the most listened-to program emanating from the main studios on State Street, with Eddie instituting Polish skits with theater personalities from Chicago," *Polish Cavalcade of Music* host Wally Skibinski wrote in a history of the station. Oskierko continued the program for fifty-two years before retiring due to poor health. That program spun off the *Tony Piet Amateur Hour*, which showcased local musicians on Sundays. Oskierko broadcasted more Polish-language events like a Christmas Midnight Mass at St. Casimir in Hammond. Skibinski started on *Polish Musical Varieties* after being encouraged to apply at Cavalier Inn in Hammond and went on to start *Polish Cavalcade of Music*, which became one of the longest continuously broadcasted shows in the United States and earned him a long-running role as master of ceremonies for Dyngus Day festivals and a number of accolades, such as a lifetime membership in the Pulaski Citizens Club for promoting Polish culture in the Calumet Region. His show's forty-nine-year run ended in 2001. *Aristotle of the Airwaves* host Nicholas Paravantes, an immigrant who grew up in Argos, Greece, broadcast the *Hellenic Radio Program*, a ninety-minute weekly Greek-language show that debuted in 1958 and featured music and public service announcements, such as about registering with immigration officials. "We try to keep in touch with the Greek culture," Paravantes told *The Times* in a 1978 article. "We're also trying to help those who come to this country to become good citizens and adjust to the United States." The multilingual and diverse WJOB also aired the *Spanish Program*, the *Slovak Hour*, the *Hungarian Hour* and other niche shows for different parts of the community. "Included in this schedule of programming was Eddie Honesty of *Rockin Rhythm*, the first black-oriented program on WJOB heard every Wednesday from 3:15 to 4 o'clock and also on Saturday afternoons from 2 to 3 o'clock," Skibinski wrote. "The only black newscaster in the country was heard on WJOB every Sunday at 10 a.m. In addition, the Rev. Odell Reed conducted his worship services from his church located at 4635 State Street in Chicago, becoming the first remote broadcast of the radio station WJOB."

WJOB has spawned many successful radio careers, including that of Felicia Middlebrook and Jerry Smith of WBBM in Chicago, Hugh Hill and John Gibbs at NBC 5 in Chicago and East Chicago native Frank Reynolds, who hosted *ABC Nightly News* in New York City. *A Christmas Story* author Jean Shepherd, who first made a name for himself on the airwaves in Cincinnati and New York City, got his start at WJOB, where he even called Hammond High School games. "He brought what he knew and learned from the Region with him to New York," Dedelow said. "We are keeping our Region's same traditions and voices alive and heard for new generations." WJOB nearly became a Catholic station, but the Catholic nonprofit Starboard Media Foundation's attempt to buy it in 2003 fell through. Former Hammond mayor Thomas McDermott Sr. owned the station for a time but eventually sold it a New England radio executive as part of a $9.4 million deal.

In 2014, WJOB moved to a highly visible 1,700-square-foot studio along a heavily trafficked highway at Purdue University Northwest's brand-new 18,000-square-foot Commercialization and Manufacturing Excellence Center at 7116 Indianapolis Boulevard after an investment of $250,000. "The vision for our Commercialization Center is to encourage small business development that benefits our Region," Purdue University Northwest chancellor Thomas Keon told *The Times* in 2013. "The opportunity to partner with a small, respected company and longtime friend of Purdue Calumet is appealing to our university from business and educational perspectives." Dedelow started at the radio station as an on-air personality in the 1980s before leaving to go work as a trader in Chicago. He came back to buy the station out of bankruptcy in 2004 after it was briefly an all-religious format. He's since often blogged and talked about standing out in front of the studio as the rush of traffic and countless trucks speed by. He even braved the negative-twenty-degree cold in winter of the 2019, when the wind chill whipped at fifty below zero.

"We plan to create state-of-the-art broadcast studios and relocate our streaming media center," Dedelow, who co-owned the radio station with his wife, Alexis Vazquez Dedelow, said in 2013. "In doing so, we will engage Purdue Calumet students in cutting-edge learning opportunities, which will benefit them and WJOB. We feel very good about this business opportunity." Dedelow has discussed using the old longtime location as a museum about WJOB and Region radio history. Under his leadership, the station tries to innovate to keep up with changing times; it became the first radio station in Northwest Indiana to launch a smartphone app and regularly broadcasts on Facebook Live.

Northwest Indiana has been home to a number of media outlets, including the *Post-Tribune*, the *Valparaiso Vidette-Messenger*, the *Region Sports Network*, *Northwest Indiana Life*, the *Chesterton Tribune*, WLTH, WLPR, the *LaPorte Herald-Argus*, the *Michigan City News Dispatch* and X-Rock 103.9. But Hammond has, for whatever reason, produced the Region's largest and most iconic media brands: WJOB on the air and *The Hammond Times* in print. *The Hammond Times*, now Northwest Indiana's leading media company and the second-largest newspaper in the state after the *Indianapolis Star*, long ago relocated to Munster but was an anchor of downtown Hammond for more than eight decades. The paper initially struggled to build up a readership because many of the early immigrants hailed from Germany and spoke little English. But in 1906, the rich Chicago grain and stockbroker Sidmon McHie bought *The Hammond Times* and "turned the paper around, using it to promote Lake County's young industries and businesses," according to the Indiana State Library's *Hoosier State Chronicles*.

Under the leadership of legendary editor Bill Nangle, *The Times* eclipsed the long-dominant *Gary Post-Tribune* in circulation and was named the best newspaper in the state multiple times by the Hoosier State Press Association during the 1990s. Rebranded as *The Times of Northwest Indiana*, it became the leading newspaper in the Northwest Indiana market, surpassing 100,000 in print circulation. The storied newspaper published many greats like the acclaimed columnist Mark Kiesling and the Indiana Sports Journalism Hall of Fame inductee Al Hamnick, known for his frequent interviews with

Merrillville native and San Antonio Spurs coach Gregg Popovich and his fondness for McDonald's coffee. In its early days, *The Hammond Times* helped spawn Edwin Fitzgerald, the "millionaire newsboy" who hawked papers at commuter train stations and in quiet residential neighborhoods. Fitzgerald and his bombastic assistant "Hymie" Weiss sold papers with cries like "The Germans are coming! The Germans are coming! Read all about it!"

21
WOODMAR COUNTRY CLUB

Golfers first teed off at Hammond's Woodmar Country Club just south of the Calumet River in 1925 and continued to golf at the 110-acre course through 2005. The private course at 1818 177th Street was designed by Ken Killian and Dick Nugent to "challenge even the best of golfers," according to *Indiana Golf*. The landmark with its historic Tudor Revival clubhouse designed by architect L. Cosby Bernard closed after the land was sold to the outdoor superstore Cabela's, which anchored a redevelopment of the property that included a Super Walmart. "I always loved playing there and felt I was one of many who would be sad to see it go," bank marketing executive and photographer Pete Doherty told *The Times* after it closed. "At the time I was shooting some stuff for a local golf magazine and thought it would be great to photograph it and capture a piece of history." The course was so popular that Doherty published a book of his photography and exhibited his shots of Woodmar around the Region, including at South Shore Arts in Munster, the Lake County Public Library in Merrillville and the Starbucks in the former Radisson at Star Plaza in Merrillville. It was a successor to the Hammond Country Club that started in 1912 on an eighty-acre site that spilled over into West Hammond. "It became extremely popular, had a large clubhouse that is still used by the American Legion, and was sold for a redevelopment," according to the *Hammond, Indiana American Bicentennial Yearbook*.

The membership was quick to migrate over to the Woodmar Country Club in the southeastern part of the city. "The first organization only had

The Woodmar Country Club was a destination for golfers throughout Northwest Indiana. *Hammond Public Library.*

The Woodmar Country Club was a hub for socializing. *Hammond Public Library.*

nine holes, plus a somewhat awkward layout and thus its membership transferred to the new site of 18 holes," the yearbook stated. Unlike with its predecessor, the decision to close the Woodmar Country Club was hotly contested with country club members voting 80–69 to sell the property for $14 million just after Halloween. Jim Romar, the golf pro at Woodmar for thirty-one years, told *The Times* it was sad to see the club the sale of a club that often hosted the Hammond Rotary Club and many community banks.

"The saddest thing is that Hammond is going to lose its country club," he said. "To me, it's an important part of the community. Hammond won't realize the loss for a few years, but it will. They [employees] will all scatter for jobs. They have to make a living." Members also scattered around to various golf courses throughout the Region, President Mary Kaczka told *The Times*. "We went and toured six different sites to move our meetings," Kaczka said. "Our club will stay in South Hammond. All the sites we looked at are in that area. It's hard to find a place like that [Woodmar]. Our members are very spoiled. It is a beautiful facility, and we have been treated very well. We feel like we were spoiled. But they made their decision and we'll have to move." After the Woodmar Country Club was razed, Cabela's built a 250,000-square-foot superstore with a mountain, aquarium and museum-grade taxidermy, which has proven to be a major draw to the city's south side.

22

WOODMAR MALL

The last vestiges of Hammond's Woodmar Mall, once a suburban frontier that drew away from downtown's retail hub but itself became abandoned in the scorched-earth population shift ever outward, vanished in 2018. It was a classic that had been inducted into the Mall Hall of Fame. "Eight inline stores held a collective grand opening in the spring of 1954, with the remaining eighteen beginning business in May of the same year," the Mall Hall of Fame posted on its website. "The $3 million dollar complex was anchored by a 2-level (65,000 square foot), Chicago-based Carson Pirie Scott. The store, which was the chain's second branch location and the first Carson's in Indiana, opened November 1, 1954." After the closure, Hammond took down the iconic Woodmar sign on Indianapolis Boulevard, and the three-story Carson's, the last store left standing, shuttered after its parent company, the Bon-Ton Stores, filed for bankruptcy. It was picked clean during a months-long liquidation sale; only a few fixtures, toilet paper boxes and odd cologne bottles remained in the end.

Built in 1954 at Indianapolis Boulevard and 165th Street in what came to be known as the Woodmar neighborhood, Woodmar was constructed by Chicago-based Landau & Heyman and designed by Austrian socialist Victor Gruen, a pioneering architect who designed more than fifty shopping malls across the United States from the 1950s to the 1970s. Woodmar was one his first, and some said it showed, with hallways that abruptly ended and a red neon strip that said Woodmar over and over in the food court. The Hammond Historical Society described the mall in the *Flashback*:

Shoppers long flocked to the Woodmar Mall in Hammond. *Hammond Public Library.*

Carson's unique architectural design, in the shape of a pentagon, was the first five-side department store built in the United State. It was a radical departure from the usual block style buildings being built. Carson's was also the first building in Lake County to have escalators or moving stairways. The original store was only two floors, a third floor that as added when the mall was enclosed in 1964/1965. The two-story building contained 65,000 square feet and went to 115,000 square feet when the third floor was added. The story was completely air conditioned and utilized as a water saving system in its air conditioning system to help conserve water during Hammond's critical summer months.

Originally, Woodmar started out as an open-air, V-shaped mall that Santa would visit by helicopter. It was anchored by a Carson Pirie Scott, a J.J. Newberry Variety Store and a National Supermarket with an igloo out front. It was later enclosed in the mid-1960s because it was the prevalent trend of the era—and to protect shoppers from the noxious odors of nearby plants. The Carson's was given a third floor, taking it from 65,000 square feet to 115,000 square feet. The mall became home to Woodmar Records, a Purdue Calumet University bookstore, an arcade, a Schoop's, the Court

LOST HAMMOND, INDIANA

Shoppers browse through the Carson's at the Woodmar Mall. *Hammond Public Library.*

of Lions and the Court of Turtles, where shoppers tossed coins into a fountain with three ceramic turtle sculptures. Generations of Region kids went there to see Santa or the Easter Bunny. People shopped at stores like Kay Bee Toys, Fannie May, Lerner New York, Foot Locker and Armstrong Jewelers. It drew visitors with a fifty-mile health walk and a helicopter drop of marshmallow Easter eggs. Traffic at the mall began to decline when the 1.3-million-square-foot River Oaks Center opened in neighboring Calumet City, and the super-regional Southlake Mall, the second-largest enclosed shopping center in the state of Indiana, opened down the road in Hobart. J.J. Newberry and the National Supermarket both closed in the late 1970s and were replaced with the somewhat eccentric Court of Lions and Court of Turtles wings that opened up more retail space for smaller shops.

The owners aspired to triple the size and add two more anchors, but a recession and high interest rates dashed their dreams. In the early 2000s, only a dozen businesses remained open and urban wear stores started cropping up. A Mexican restaurant, the first new business to open there in years, established a foothold in the food court but swiftly went under, failing in less than six months. On the Labelscar retail history blog, a visitor in 2000 described Woodmar as "almost deserted, ghostly, yet somehow pristinely beautiful." *The Times of Northwest Indiana* business writer Andrea Holecek

Lost Hammond, Indiana

The Woodmar Mall drew shoppers away from downtown. *Hammond Public Library.*

vividly described it as "a graveyard of empty stores and silent corridors" with a "parking lot filled with potholes instead of autos" and "halls studded with buckets collecting rainwater from leaky ceilings." Times got so hard they even shut the water off to the turtle fountain. "The Carson Pirie Scott store occupies 50 percent of the mall's 230,000 square feet and keeps it on life support," she wrote. Labelscar blogger Prange Way, who tried to visit every mall in the Chicago metropolitan area, marveled at how vintage and eccentric it was, feeling like a "paleontologist unearthing the strata of time":

> *This mall was by far the most remarkable that I saw in the Chicago area, with so many notable and fascinating design features. The first visible attribute upon entering the site—the mall's anchor, Carson Pirie Scott, is an amazingly huge behemoth—a relic of a dinosaur in terms of the size of anchors built onto malls today. Inside the mall, the throwbacks to the past continue. Immediately upon entering from one of two Carson's entrances to Center Court, my sense of smell overtook me—people were smoking in the mall. Lots of people. I haven't seen smoking allowed in a mall since I was a kid—probably 15 years ago now, and there were numerous Carson's employees as well as customers sitting around smoking. Throughout the mall, there were numerous people loitering, just smoking*

on benches. What an odd sight. Also at center court, the mall's name is inscribed in red cursive writing along the top of the ceiling, simply reading "woodmarwoodmarwoodmar"—over and over.

The Woodmar Mall ended up going bankrupt, and David Fesco purchased in 2003 with high hopes of revitalizing the property as a fashion outlet center like the Dixie Outlet Mall in suburban Toronto. After that project failed, the City of Hammond and Northbrook, Illinois–based Praedium Development Corp. eyed a total makeover that would transform the "nearly empty mall into a central commercial zone," according to *The Times*. But the lack of maintenance and investment in the property over the years proved to be too much to overcome. Leaky roofs, sewage problems and uncertainty among tenants over the mall's future precipitated its ultimate demise. Prange Way saw the death of the half-century-old mall as a symbol of something more, society's tendency to cast everything aside in a push toward more distant suburbs:

> *Woodmar Mall represents more than the end of a retail era, or even the sentimentality associated with it. Certainly such things are important, but the bigger picture eludes to problems on a broader scale. What can Woodmar Mall teach us about urban sprawl, using space efficiently, and even environmental sustainability? Land ecology and urban planning aside, what implications does this have on our throwaway society and the "American way"? Some may say that this indicates merely a natural economic cycle, and that it's fine. They wash their hands at the notion that blight and urban sprawl are more than socio-economic problems, but environmental ones as well. Others say that these are legitimate problems, that will eventually catch up with us and by washing our hands of these problems, we'll never get them clean.*

Hammond tore down the mall in 2006, but Carson's persisted as a standalone department store along with the Barbasol-like Woodmar sign straight out of the 1950s. Carson's parent company, the Bon-Ton Stores, long looked at moving to a smaller one-story storefront nearby and declared bankruptcy in 2018, closing its sixty-four-year-old three-story store after a lengthy liquidation sale. Shortly after the store closed for good in August, the new $17 million, state-of-the-art Hammond SportsPlex opened next door. It offered indoor basketball courts, volleyball courts and soccer fields for youth sports, and Hammond mayor Thomas McDermott preferred the idea of razing the old department store instead of trying to salvage it to make way for more complementary development such as hotels and restaurants for the visiting families. "It's unfortunate, but I prefer to look toward the future, not the past," he said.

23
HAMMOND PROS AND OTHER PROFESSIONAL SPORTS

The Hammond Pros were one of the earliest National Football League teams, but they never played in Hammond and weren't really professionals. The team never played a home game in its namesake city since it lacked a field with adequate seating. The Pros playing most of their home games in a neighboring Chicago stadium now known as Wrigley Field. And it paid so little most players held full-time jobs elsewhere and had little time to practice.

George Halas, the legendary owner of the Chicago Bears who went on to define its defensive, smashmouth style of football, played for the Hammond Pros for seventy-five dollars a game in 1919 before defecting the following year to the Decatur Staleys, which went on to become the Chicago Bears, according to the Hammond High School Class of 1959 city history website. Paul Parduhn and Dr. Alva Young founded the team, which was also known as the Hammond All Stars, that squared off against the Cleveland Tigers, the Toledo Maroons, the Canton Bulldogs, the Detroit Heralds and many other foes in the American Professional Football Association, a precursor to the NFL. A game against Canton that drew twelve thousand spectators proved the viability of a professional football league.

The Hammond Pros started out as a charter member of the American Professional Football Association, which became the National Football League in 1920. After seven years, the Pros put up an ignominious record of 5 wins, 26 losses and 4 ties. Midwestern Professional Champions Head and "Unofficial Founder of the National Football League" Paul Parduhn and

The Hammond Pros were one of the National Football League's earliest teams. *Hammond Public Library.*

Dr. Alva Young, a semi-pro Hammond Clabby Athletic Association football doctor, racing stable owner and boxing promoter, founded the American Professional Football Association team. Though they practiced at Turner Field at Calumet Avenue and Michigan Street on the Grand Calumet River in Hammond, they played most of their games in Cubs Park, what's now known as Wrigley Field or on the road.

"Hammond lacked an adequate field, so the Pros played their games outside Indiana," *The Times of Northwest Indiana* Sports Editor Ryan Nilsson wrote. "The players on the Pros held day jobs and as a result struggled against teams like George Halas' Decatur Staleys." The team did make history by having the National Football League's first black coach, Hall of Famer Fritz Pollard, while also fielding six of the league's nine African American players at the time. Halas and John "Paddy" Driscoll, who was one of the top quarterbacks and halfbacks in the early days of the NFL for the Pros, Chicago Bears and Chicago Cardinals, also were enshrined in the Hall of Fame in Canton, Ohio. Driscoll was a triple threat, one of the best drop-kickers in football, and made the NFL's all-1920s team. He played a single season with the Pros.

Originally the Hammond All-Stars, the team was dissolved in 1926 when the NFL scrapped smaller franchises after defeating the American Football League in a heated rivalry, contracting to just twelve teams. "It can be argued the Pros' chief contribution to the NFL was fielding teams with black athletes, according to an article on the Pro Football Researchers Association website," Nilsson wrote. "Black stars such as Fred 'Fritz' Pollard, Jay 'Inky' Williams, John Shelburne and Sol Butler played for Hammond." Hall of Famer Pollard was the first black coach in the NFL when he led the Pros, was one of the first two African American players in the league, was an All-American and was "one of the greatest runners these eyes have ever seen." "Before his name became synonymous with diversity in professional football, before he went into the Hall of Fame, Pollard led the Hammond Pros across this field next to the Calumet River. He was the quarterback, the running back, the kicker. He was the punter and the defensive back. He was the coach," *Indianapolis Star* columnist Gregg Doyel wrote. "People say he ran like Barry Sanders or Gale Sayers, that kind of elusiveness. One person went so far as to call 5-8, 155-pound Fritz Pollard 'one of the great ones.' Maybe you've heard of the guy who said that: Red Grange."

In an age of discrimination, Pollard had to get dressed in the cigar store of the owner when he played in Akron. "A tough man, Fritz Pollard," Doyel wrote. "Had to be, to break professional football's color barrier. He needed an occasional police escort to walk safely onto the field, and when he played in Akron he couldn't dress in the stadium with the rest of the team. And he wasn't just the team's best player—he was the Akron coach too."

In addition to some of the sport's early legends, the Pros boasted an enormous offensive line dubbed the "Hammond Hippos," but won only five games in seven seasons against opposition that ranged from the Green Bay Packers to the semipro Gary Elks and the Kokomo American Legion team, once squaring off against the legendary Olympic hero Jim Thorpe, who was reportedly twenty pounds overweight and had whiskey breath. The team was out of the league by 1917, when the smaller markets started to get drummed out. Little today is left to commemorate the Hammond Pros, which were last a part of the city more than ninety years ago. McDermott, whose father also was mayor of Hammond, said he had never heard of them until after he was elected and was emailed an old newspaper clipping about a game between the Pros and the Green Bay Packers. "People taught me about Hammond's history," McDermott told *The Times*. "But I bet 98 percent of Hammond residents didn't even realize that we used to have an NFL team in Hammond. This is going to be good to remind people that our city has a proud history. And we've been around a long time." As a tribute to Hammond's history as one of the original NFL towns, the league announced the Los Angeles Chargers' sixth-round draft pick during a live telecast at the Hammond Sportsplex in 2019. The team that abandoned San Diego for a half-filled soccer stadium about two hours north in the City of Angels selected Houston linebacker Emeke Egbule with the 200th pick in the draft.

PRO BASKETBALL

In addition to a professional football team that never had a venue large enough for home games, Hammond was home to two early professional basketball teams: the Hammond Ciesar All-Americans and the Hammond Calumet Buccaneers. Legendary UCLA coach John Wooden played for the Ciesar All-Americans in the Hammond Civic Center. The National Basketball League team squared off against the likes of the New York Celtics, a defunct team that disbanded during World War I and had no relation to the Boston Celtics. The Ciesar All-Americans played in Whiting and Hammond from 1935 to 1941, earning a single playoff berth in which the team lost in the semifinals. University of Toledo collegiate star Chuck Chuckovitz briefly played for the team before the owner started withholding paychecks and went on to Toledo where he earned the Most Valuable Player award with a league-leading 18.5 points per game. Then in the 1948–49 season, its sole campaign in the National Basketball League, the Hammond Calumet Buccaneers racked up a 21-41 record. Despite the atrocious .339 winning percentage, they entered the playoffs, only to be unceremoniously knocked out in the first round by the Syracuse Nationals. The team played home games at the 4,500-seat Hammond Civic Center against teams like the Detroit Vagabond Kings and the Oshkosh All-Stars.

BOXING

On top of pro and prep sports, and the robust Hammond Sports Hall of Fame that enshrines athletic greats in the halls of the Hammond Civic Center, Hammond has been a hub for boxing. Boxing once was ubiquitous

Circuses often visited the Hammond Civic Center, which also has long been a major hub for boxing in the Region. *Hammond Public Library.*

in the Civic Center, where boxers traded blows, at one time against title contenders like East Chicago native Angel Manfredy who won hearts and souls with the El Diablo persona in which he wore a latex devil mask before entering the ring during the HBO fight nights of the 1990s and early 2000s, a period in which he was one of the most popular fighters and recorded most of his wins by knockout. The floor was once sticky with spilled beer, the cards once contaminated with long-irrelevant sluggers. Only cops and boxers fight there now, before dwindling crowds of spectators. The Hammond Civic Center hosted popular acts during the 1970s, including KISS, Styx and Cheech and Chong. Protesters objected to KISS's concert, which seems quaint and almost unimaginable in the modern day when the heavily stylized band has burger restaurants in airports and retail trade areas across the country.

WRESTLING

Hammond also spawned one of the premier professional wrestling families in all of history: the Funks. Dory Funk won the Indiana state high school championship three years in a row for Hammond High School and was the Indiana State University Amateur Athletic Union champion before becoming a professional wrestler in the Texas Territories, winning the National Wrestling Association Heavyweight Championship in 1969, squaring off against the likes of Iron Mike DiBiase, the adoptive father of Ted "The Million Dollar Man" DiBiase.

Like many Region residents, Dory Funk worked at Inland Steel on a summer home from college and at the Pullman-Standard Manufacturing plant making tanks. He immersed himself in wrestling and his studies in high school after getting scared straight during a brush with the Chicago Outfit. "One summer, between my father's freshman and sophomore years in high school, Dory Funk had what he thought was a great idea—he would slug a few slots in the syndicated-owned stories in Calumet City," his son Terry Funk wrote in his autobiography *More Than Just Hardcore*. "Their plan was that my father's buddy would distract the store clerk, while my father would push slugs into the slot machines. He did well for about half an hour." But the clerk eventually caught on to the scheme. "Dory pushed him aside and ran out of the store, knowing the mob would be after him and knowing they wouldn't care that he as only a kid, or who his old man was." He skipped town and rode the rails for much of the summer but returned home before school started and was initially mistaken as a bum in the alley. His parents burned his filthy clothes in a trash can. "Adam asked why he had run away. When Dory told him about getting caught slugging the slot machines, Adam took off his belt and gave him the beating of a lifetime," Terry Funk and his coauthor Scott E. Williams wrote. "The next morning, Adam and Dory took a father-son trip to Calumet City. They went to the store, where Adam made Dory apologize for what had happened weeks earlier. Dory also promised to repay every penny he had bilked from the store. Then Adam told everyone in the store, 'If you harm my boy in any way you'll have hell to pay.'"

Dory Funk went on to become a wrestling great, grappling with the original Gorgeous George before seven thousand people at the Dick Bivens Stadium in Amarillo and winning a ninety-minute long Texas Death Match against Mike DiBiase to be crowned "King of the Death Match." A master of the spinning toe hold, he was known for blending brawling with jiujitsu and endurance matches that sometimes went on for hours in the West

Texas territory. An NWA World Junior Heavyweight champion, he was inducted into the George Tragos/Lou Thesz Professional Wrestling Hall of Fame at the International Wrestling Institute and Museum in Iowa, perhaps the biggest hotbed of amateur wrestling in the United States, after dying of a heart attack at the age of fifty-four while demonstrating a wrestling hold at his home.

He fathered hardcore legend Terry Funk and Dory Funk Jr., who invented the Texas cloverleaf submission hold and ran the professional wrestling school the Funking Conservatory, producing wrestling superstars like Matt Hardy, Jeff Hardy, Edge and Kurt Angle. Dory Funk Jr. won a number of championships, was the fifth-longest reigning NWA World Heavyweight Champion of all time and was inducted into the WWE Hall of Fame. Terry Funk, who wrestled under various stage names like Black Baron, Chainsaw Charlie, Dr. Knows-it-All and the Texan, made a name for himself with suplexes, forearm smashes and spinning toe holds against competitors like Harley Race, Ric Flair, Cactus Jack, Bruiser Brody, Junkyard Dog, Wild Bull Curry, Tommy Dreamer and Tito Santana. He wrestled for many promotions, including the World Wrestling Federation, Extreme Championship Wrestling, All Japan Pro Wrestling, the National Wrestling Alliance, World Championship Wrestling, the International Wrestling Association of Japan and Frontier Martial-Arts Wrestling. He's been inducted into many halls of fame, including the NWA, WCW and WWE. The legend has appeared in *Beyond the Mat*, *Over the Top*, *Road House*, *Friday Night Lights*, *Quantum Leap*, *Swamp Thing* and the eminently memeable *Beyond Belief: Fact or Fiction*—he even coordinated the final fight scene in *Rocky V*.

From the WWE Hall of Fame:

> *Younger brother Terry debuted in 1965 captured the NWA World Championship 10 years later, thus making the Funks the only brothers to have held that prestigious honor. When he wasn't teaming with Dory Jr., Terry also competed in singles matches across the country, continuing to make a name for himself globally. Interestingly, the Funk brothers' in-ring styles were polar opposites of each other. Whereas Dory Jr. relied on savvy, finesse and skill, Terry started that way but developed into more of a deliberate brawler who became controversial, to say the least, by targeting Ric Flair in WCW. In the mid-1990s, "The Funker" would gain a new fanbase, thanks heavily to his tenure with ECW as well as a brief return stint in WWE as "Chainsaw Charlie." This new chapter in his career*

made him a hardcore icon. So no matter what individual or collective roads were traveled through the years by Dory Funk Jr. and Terry Funk, both men have deservedly stamped their brand into the WWE Hall of Fame.

24
HAMMOND DISTILLING COMPANY

More than a century before the popular and acclaimed craft brewery 18th Street Brewing opened a distillery in downtown Hammond in 2018, the M.M. Towle Distilling Company started making whiskey in a four-story building in 1883. Towle founded the business with $150,000 in capital, A.T. Andreas wrote in *A History of Hammond*. Hammond's first distillery originally made both corn syrup and whiskey but switched to the more profitable liquor when federal law prohibited doing any other business in a building where distilling takes place. It went on to employ 25 workers and produce 3,000 barrels of liquor per day. Then the Hammond Distilling Company opened on the southeast corner of Calumet Avenue and 150th Street just north of the Grand Calumet River in 1901. It grew its capacity until it could produce 50,000 gallons of whiskey per day and paying more than $120,000 in tax revenue per year, making it one of America's largest distilleries at the time. Built for $500,000, the Hammond Distillery generated $6 million a year in revenue and placed its general manager, John Fitzpatrick, on the Chicago Board of Trade because of its heavy consumption of grain. It closed because of America's failed flirtation with Prohibition in 1918 and was ultimately turned into a feed mill by the Nowak Milling corporation of Buffalo. "Before Prohibition killed the Hammond Distillery, it was arguably the second largest in Indiana, cranking out 25,000 to perhaps 50,000 gallons of alcoholic beverages daily," *The Times of Northwest*

Lost Hammond, Indiana

The Hammond Distillery was the second largest in the nation before Prohibition. *Hammond Public Library.*

Indiana reporter Doug Ross wrote. "In *The Lake County Times'* first issue, on June 18, 1906, the Hammond Distillery said it had a capacity of 25,000 gallons daily, offering Hammond Bourbon, Hammond Sourmash, Hammond Rye Malt Gin, Hammond Dry Gin, Cologne Spirits and Refined Alcohol."

In 1909, the Hammond Distillery added a plant that allowed its dry slop, a byproduct of the distilling process, to be shipped to farms for cattle feed instead of keeping cattle on the premises to consume it on-site. Rumors circulated that the legendary gangster Al Capone shipped the distillery's liquor across the state line to fuel his organized crime empire after the distillery went under. He was rumored to have bought its remaining inventory when Prohibition started. "There's this mythology that organized crime in the greater Chicago area, in Northwest Indiana, had to all been linked to Capone," Jason Lantzer, assistant director of the University Honors Program at Butler University in Indianapolis, told *The Times of Northwest Indiana.* "And there's enough truth to that in that you do have definite Capone-owned or -operated outfits and purchases of different things, and it became very easy to mythologize that that was also by Capone. Whether or not we ever will be able figure out it was or not. But if had to do with organized crime it must have been linked to Al Capone." The mythology spread by word of mouth. "This building was around in the 1920s, so it must have been used by Capone, or there are these stories that they were used by organized crime. Whether that actually happened, I don't know, but that's what I've been told, or that my uncle's cousin told him that Capone came here on vacation or something," Lantzer added. "There's a story that Capone owned or ran bootleg liquor out of the Paramount Theater in Hammond. Whether or not that's true, I have no idea." Capone certainly could have used the Hammond Distillery as a production facility during Prohibition, Lantzer told *The Times*:

> *The problem wasn't the availability of things. If you've got corn, yeast and some sugar and can fashion a still, you can make yourself some alcohol. The problem was whether it would be good. Or whether you would kill your customers, because that doesn't really breed a lot of confidence and repeat confidence when it gets around that Joe down the street bought from you and he's dead now because he drank what you made. Maybe it's fun to attach it to Capone, but maybe it's a way to say that wasn't really us, that was an outside element. I think that is something for the 1920s that we need more study on.*

After Prohibition took effect and the saloons formerly owned by breweries were converted into ice cream parlors, it limped on with a contract to produce alcohol to make smokeless gunpowder during World War I. Prohibition agent Robert Anderson was shot to death there in 1923 after repeated thefts of whiskey barrels. Twenty armed bandits made off with thousands of dollars of liquor the following year. Efforts were made to restart the Hammond Distillery after Prohibition ended, but they never got off the ground. Whiskey prices plunged, and the distillery got delisted from the Chicago Board of Trade, making it difficult to line up financing. Owner Maxwell Nowak told *The Times* he was unable to turn a profit. The Nowak Milling Corporation moved its feed mill to the other side of the property, and the Hammond Distillery ended up closing for good.

Today, 18th Street Distillery, named after the business corridor in Chicago's Pilsen neighborhood where owner and "Overlord" Drew Fox once lived, opened in a former warehouse building downtown with a

Great Gatsby theme, serving up craft cocktails with rye, bourbon, gin and moonshine. The spinoff of 18th Street Brewery won six medals at the American Distilling Institute's Craft Spirits Awards in Colorado in 2019, including Rye Whiskey, Bourbon, Pot Still Rum, Contemporary Gin, 100 Proof Rye Whiskey and Barrel Proof Rye Whiskey. "People from all over our state and country who visit us at our Hammond location are able to enjoy our spirits via our tasting lounge which has an incredible cocktail program," Fox told *The Times of Northwest Indiana.* "Northwest Indiana can no longer be ignored when it comes to manufacturing award-winning distilled spirits."

18th Street operates a campus of craft beer and artisan spirits downtown that includes the distillery's cocktail lounge, the offshoot Sour Note Brewing taproom and its own heavy metal–themed brewpub. *USA Today 10 Best* named 18th Street the best brewpub in the nation, which Fox said would help draw more tourists to Hammond and Gary's lakefront Miller Beach neighborhood. "With over 7,300 breweries in the country, we are completely shocked, humbled and honored to be recognized as America's Best Brewpub of 2019 by *USA Today*'s Top 10," Fox said. "This is a big deal for tourism for the cities of Hammond and Gary, Indiana. Both locations are flanked by major interstate and toll roads which allows easy access for drivers to reach our brewpubs to enjoy our awesome beers and food." Hammond's booze-making tradition also extends to beer. A favorite among German immigrants, Hammond Beer was brewed by the Hammond Brewing Company between 1890 and 1918. Its signs hung outside many of the early taverns and saloons in town. German brewer George M. Eder and local bottler Charles H. Mayer put out beers like Bohemian Lager and Muhlhauser Export. *Nuvo Newsweekly* craft beer writer Rita Kohn noted the Hammond Brewing Company was the city's only brewery until 3 Floyds came around with a five-barrel system in 1996. Brothers Nick and Simon Floyd and their father, Mike Floyd, started a brewery that would go on to be rated best in the world multiple years in a row while "armed with only a few hundred dollars, a five-barrel Frankenstein wok-burner-fired brew kettle, repurposed open Swiss cheese fermenters (Hammond Squares) and an Old Canfield's Cola tank," according to the 3 Floyds website. The brewery's "It's Not Normal" ales and lagers took Chicagoland by storm, ending up on seemingly every tap across the city and on murals behind liquor stores in Chicago's Jefferson Park neighborhood. After only four years in Hammond, the heavy metal–themed craft brewery known of its aggressive hops and chef-driven gastropub menus relocated to a sleepy industrial park tucked away in neighboring Munster to the south, where it was named the world's best craft brewery by *RateBeer* multiple times over. Though 3 Floyds has decamped, the city's brewing tradition continues at 18th Street Brewing downtown and Byway Brewing in Oxbow Landing by the Borman Expressway, which was named Indiana Brewery of the Year during the Indiana Brewers Cup Competition in Indianapolis in 2016.

25

BANK CALUMET AND OTHER FINANCIAL INSTITUTIONS

The Hoosier State Bank in Hammond was famously robbed in 1955 by then-twenty-six-year-old James "Whitey" Bulger, the Boston mob moss who made away with $12,612 from the tellers' drawers after wielding a pistol in each hand while his accomplice hopped the counter, according to the *Boston Globe*. Bulger, who was murdered in federal prison in 2018 after being portrayed in films by A-list actors like Jack Nicholson and Johnny Depp, reportedly celebrated the heist in neighboring Chicago. It was the first time that Bulger, a notorious snitch, attracted the attention of the Federal Bureau of Investigation.

"[His accomplice] Carl Smith had once lived in Hammond, Ind., and that was why Bulger's next bank job was there. Smith had identified a bank in the Midwest town as a soft touch," Kevin Cullen and Shelley Murphy wrote in the *Boston Globe*. "Smith, Bulger and another accomplice, Richard Barchard, drove out to rob it on October 29, 1955, but backed off when they saw a police officer stationed inside. As they left Hammond, Bulger and Barchard noticed another bank in town that looked like an easy mark." They headed back to the Northeast, where Bulger robbed a suburban Boston bank; he vaulted over the counter and snatched more than $5,000 out of the tellers' drawers. "Bulger and Barchard decided to leave town to let the heat die down," Cullen and Murphy continued. "They remembered the lonely little bank in Hammond, Ind., and decided to make it a double date. Barchard took his wife, Dorothy, and Bulger brought Jacqui McAuliffe along. The boys left the girls in a motel and cased

The Bank Calumet tower has long been an anchor of downtown Hammond though Bank Calumet successor First Midwest Bank abandoned it as part of its "Delivering Excellence" cost-cutting scheme. *Hammond Public Library.*

the bank, then hit it the next day, Nov. 23, 1955." Bulger was armed with two handguns and pistol-whipped a customer to the chest, shoving him to the floor. Police later arrested Smith, who started to talk and identified Bulger as one of the robbers. Hammond police got a warrant for Bulger's arrest, and he went and hid out in California before he was eventually arrested by the Federal Bureau of Investigations at a Boston nightclub in 1956, which is when he first cooperated with authorities.

At one time home to many homegrown banks, Hammond was long a financial services hub for Northwest Indiana, which at one time had fifty-one community banks, a number that's dwindled greatly over the years as larger, often out-of-state financial institutions have snapped them up. Hammond lost all of its early banks, including the State Bank of Hammond, when they all failed during the Great Depression. It became the largest city in the United States without a bank when the State Bank of Hammond liquidated in 1932, according to the Hammond Public Library. "In desperation, Mayor Charles Schonert, along with Thomas Tennat, president of the Chamber of Commerce, assisted by Joseph Hirsch, head of the Merchants Association, set up a currency exchange in the lobby of the failed First Trust & Savings Bank," Archibald McKinlay wrote in his Region Roots column. "Hammond bank failures were a particular problem for L.L. Caldwell, school superintendent, who had to meet a $75,000 payroll but had $500,000 locked up in the Hammond National Bank alone. By way of treading water, he resorted to a variety of tricks, including tax anticipation warrants, post-dated checks and scrip. His crisis would last several years." Hammond's plight became national news. "This attracted the attention of Mercantile Bank, which came to town and opened for business" in 1932, according to the *History of the Hammond Public Library*. It was followed shortly thereafter by Bank Calumet, which grew into one of the largest banks ever headquartered in Hammond, expanding to twenty-nine branches, including one hundred sites in local grocery stores like Meijer. Its office towered over downtown Hammond.

But in 2006, Itasca-based First Midwest Bank bought out Bank Calumet for $309 million. Bank Calumet liked that First Midwest has a similar culture and business model, while First Midwest liked that Bank Calumet's Lake County business was demographically similar to its base in suburban Chicago. "I think in the final analysis, this is a community-run organization and they liked our culture fit better," First Midwest president and chief executive officer John O'Meara told *The Times of Northwest Indiana*. "Our money had to be there, of course, but they seemed to repeat over and over again that a company like First Midwest was more appealing to them than a larger more money-centered bank." After the merger, First Midwest ended up with $8.3 billion, loans of $4.9 billion and deposits of $6.1 billion, propelling it to be the eleventh-largest bank in Chicagoland.

Lake Federal Savings on Kennedy Avenue and 171st Street in Hammond's Hessville neighborhood also got swallowed up by a larger bank, the 102-year-old First Savings Bank of Hegewisch. The last remaining mutual savings bank in Lake County, or bank owned by its members, Lake Federal Savings amassed assets of $65 million, opening branches in Highland and St. John before getting bought out. The bank endured for nearly six decades, following its customer base into the south suburbs and maintaining a policy of fiscal prudence. Lake Federal maintained 20 percent of its capital in reserve when it was only required to maintain 8 percent. "We did pretty good as the only survivor when everyone else closed or merged," Lake Federal chairman Gerald Skrabala told *The Times of Northwest Indiana*. "Community banks are really geared and structured toward borrowers and savers, where all the decisions are locally made. We survived through prudent management. We maintained asset quality and were competitive with the interest rates." Still, Skrabala decided to retire in 2013 after more than two decades with the bank. "It's just time," he told *The Times*. "I want to be like John Wayne in the cowboy movies and ride off into the sunset." First Federal Savings and Loans, which had branches on Rimbach Street in downtown Hammond and Cline Avenue in Highland, made its exit in 2013 when it was purchased by Peoples Bank. First Federal had total assets of $40.7 million, loans of $31.8 million and deposits of $37.6 million. The downtown Hammond-based bank had sought a buyer for more than a year. "Our goal this past year has been to explore possible relationships that would be meaningful to our customers, employees and the community," President and Chief Executive Officer John Freyek said. "We're excited to partner with Peoples and provide our customers access to a full range of deposit, lending and wealth management product and service options while preserving our community banking roots."

26
INDIANA BOTANIC GARDENS

Hammond resident Joseph Meyer founded the firm initially known as the Indiana Herb Gardens in his cottage by the Little Calumet River in 1910, selling herbs via mail order. The horticulturalist and herbalist traveled all over North America and Europe to study native plants and their uses, publishing the hefty four-hundred-page tome *The Herbalist* in 1918 and steering his company toward national growth. "He was an orphan in Germany and read a lot of books on plants," said Tim Cleland, Meyer's great-grandson and company president. "From there he started growing the plants." In 1925, the business in a distinctive English-gabled building just off the Borman Expressway was renamed the Indiana Botanic Gardens. Eventually, the company moved to nearby Hobart, where it more than quadrupled its workforce and continued to be operated by the Meyer family.

The Indiana Botanic Gardens was once the largest establishment of its kind" "The formidable two-story building, crowned with a sharp-angled red-tiled gables in the Elizabethan style, embraces a space of 36,000 square feet," according to *The Calumet Region Historical Guide*. "Here are the office, laboratories, shipping and stock rooms where a well-trained personnel takes care of a remarkable amount of mail orders from all over the world." Despite humble beginnings, it grew into a powerhouse at a time doctors were scarce and people sought out alternative treatments. The Meyer family initially stitched the catalogues with needles and thread. As more customers sought out its herbal remedies, the family-run business graduated to producing the slick annual periodical *The Herbalist Almanac*, which listed herbs and roots

LOST HAMMOND, INDIANA

The Indiana Botanical Gardens in Hammond sold natural remedies for a variety of ailments. *Hammond Public Library.*

for sale, outlined treatments for common ailments and offered advice on gardening. The eclectic publication ran for fifty-four years, helping build up a national following, until it was eventually discontinued in 1979.

Meyer's "herb factory," as it was popularly known, got so successful it spun off one of Hammond's biggest and most successful banks. "From a small beginning, Joseph E. Meyer developed a business into an international mail order business that yielded a mountain of checks," Archibald McKinlay wrote in his Region Roots column.

> *Since it was grossly inconvenient in 1931 and 1932 to run checks through out-of-town banks of dubious stability, Meyer decided to open his own bank. To help him, he enlisted two old friends: Charles Scott, a building contractor, and Lee Hutchinson, an owner of Calumet Auto Parts. These men introduced Meyer to Theodore Moor, formerly of the State Bank, whose building at 5444 Calumet Ave. Meyer occupied....The well-managed bank prospered immediately. By 1937, it would become a national bank known as the Calumet National Bank.*

As the business grew, thousands of herbs from farms in Dyer, the Kankakee River Valley and the twenty-five-acre Indiana Botanical Gardens

Lost Hammond, Indiana

The Borman Expressway displaced the Indiana Botanical Gardens, which have since relocated to Hobart. *Hammond Public Library.*

site on the Little Calumet River were "cured, cut, sifted and prepared for the market." A mill on the grounds produced the botanicals, and it eventually started importing herbs from all over the world. The company has now served health-conscious Americans for more than one hundred years, eventually selling more than five hundred types of nutritional supplements like its best-selling Vitamin C cream and apple cider vinegar plus that purports to help users lose weight. The botanical company that started in Hammond ended up offering vitamins, aromatherapy, homeopathy and herbal remedies in its catalogue, online and at wellness centers at local Strack & Van Til and Fagen Pharmacy stores. Loose teas once were the biggest seller, but business has long since shifted to vitamins, minerals, other supplements sold in pill form, cosmetics and skin care creams, Cleland told *The Times*. The business experienced rapid growth in the early 1990s. "We've manufactured natural cosmetics for some time," Cleland told *The Times* in 2002. "But five years ago, we found a wonderful European chemist, took a new look at the products and refined the formulation. Many of our customers are over 50 and looking for new ways to take better care of themselves." The Indiana Botanic Gardens also eventually started sourcing its herbs from suppliers instead of growing them on its own. Cosmetics eventually accounting for about 40 percent of the business. "We have 1,700 products, and over the years, sales of some of the products slide off, so we reformulate and remerchandise them," Cleland told *The Times*. "It's a hard battle but lots of fun."

Though still running in Hobart, the Indiana Botanic Gardens decamped from its hometown of Hammond decades ago. Today, Reaper's Realm, a popular haunted house, occupies the original Tudor-style Indiana Botanic Gardens building just off the Borman Expressway in Hammond.

27
THE ROLLER DOME

Teens started skating in circles at the Roller Dome Skating Rink at 714 Gostlin Street in Hammond in 1952, going on countless dates there over the next six decades. *The Times of Northwest Indiana* described the Roller Dome Skating Rink as a "a place for Region teens to socialize, skate and make friends" that let "old-school skating fans in the Region get a kick out of this blast from the past." It was also home to a cafeteria to grab a quick bite and an arcade for those who preferred to pursue more solitary pursuits. The skating rink piped in organ music for years but then started playing popular music in the 1970s, a move that helped quadruple attendance. "The best Christmas present I ever gave my father, because the kids went crazy for it here, was the Michael Jackson 'Thriller' video," owner Pamela Mitchell told *The Times*. "He had a screen and projected it on the screen, and kids just went crazy over that." The only indoor rink in Hammond invited skaters to take part in skating activities like Spotlight Couples and the Topsy Turvy Trio. It trained future roller derby participants and launched relationships that ended up in marriages. But as times and tastes changed, the kids eventually decided to "just beat it." "I used to go to the roller dome every Friday night when I was a kid and now it is old and run down," one online reviewer said in a 2005 post on Judy's Book. "They play old music and the kids are not well behaved at all. I honestly would not let my child go there by himself. I would be afraid someone would try and mess with him. The kids who hang out here look they are in gangs."

The 18,180-square-foot building underwent several transformations over the years to try to stay relevant but ultimately failed. Online reviewers dismissed it in the later years as "old-fashioned" and even "ghetto." "The popular rink closed its doors in 2008, when it was transformed into an indoor soccer venue, Roller Dome Soccer," but closed again in 2013, according to *The Times*. Auctioneer Jonathan Kraft told the paper that "there is a great amount of history in this classic hot spot." Today, Hammond no longer has a roller-skating rink and the closest one may be in Lynwood, Illinois. but the city is adding an ice-skating rink. The brand-new Ice Kube indoor facility in Hessville, a multimillion-dollar facility with the backing of some former Notre Dame hockey players, will host the Bishop Noll High School hockey team, a Purdue University Northwest intramural team, any other area hockey players looking to practice and members of the public looking to strap on ice skates.

28

JOHN DILLINGER MUSEUM

The *Chicago Sun-Times* reported in 2017 that "like its namesake, John Dillinger Museum meets its sudden, shocking end." The museum dedicated to "public enemy number one" was located for decades in the Frank Gehry–like Indiana Welcome Center on Kennedy Avenue in Hammond but was moved to the Old Courthouse in downtown Crown Point in 2015 and was shuttered just two years later. The museum that featured the famous wooden gun the Depression-era gangster used to escape jail in Crown Point in 1933 welcomed twenty thousand visitors from around the world, was featured on the Travel Channel and made national headlines. It showcased some gruesome artifacts like a death mask and his tombstone, which was removed from the famed Crown Hill cemetery in Indianapolis after too many people chipped off bits as grisly souvenirs.

Perhaps to preemptively deflect criticism that it glorified a murderous bank robber who was revered in his day as a folk hero despite a propensity for violence, the museum adopted the slogan "crime doesn't pay." It chronicled the gangster's well-documented exploits without glorifying them. "The John Dillinger Museum showcased a collection of historic artifacts and followed the life and times of Depression Era gangsters and the rise of the FBI during their crime sprees," the museum said on its website. "A special memorial was placed inside the museum to honor local law enforcement officers that have given their lives in the line of duty." But even local law enforcement agencies have looked to capitalize off Dillinger's notoriety. For instance, the Porter County Sheriff's Office showcases a tommy gun recovered from the

Dillinger Gang upon request, such as at a dedication of the Centier Bank Building in downtown Gary that included dignitaries like then-Indiana governor and future vice president Mike Pence.

Groupon had previously described it as a "must-see museum" that was "among the treasures of Hammond." The museum opened in Hammond in 1999 after the Hammond-based South Shore Convention and Visitors Bureau bought the collection from the estate of a Dillinger Museum based in Nashville, Indiana, between Bloomington and Columbus, according to *The Times of Northwest Indiana*. The interactive exhibit focused on history, excavation and advances in crime-fighting technology that made it harder to stick up banks, putting Dillinger's crew out of business. Many of the more gruesome artifacts related to Dillinger came from the estate of the late Joe Pinkston, an eccentric collector who opened a Dillinger Museum in his hometown of Nashville, Indiana. Pinkston put forth the theory that Dillinger was actually a good guy who was paid to rob banks by Depression-era bankers who didn't have the money to cover their accounts. Pinkston operated his museum for twenty years until his death. The Lake County Visitors and Convention Board acquired the collection and opened the museum in the Indiana Welcome Center in 1999.

When in Hammond, the museum advanced a more straightforward, factually accurate narrative about how Dillinger hit up banks around the Midwest during a time of economic turmoil. The roughly two-thousand-square-foot museum featured items like a 1933 Hudson Essex Terraplane 8 car that illustrated how Dillinger and his accomplices so easily outran the police. It closed on the eightieth anniversary of his death before relocating to Crown Point where visits rose despite it being more out of the way. "The museum described Dillinger's life and times chronologically, using artifacts, copies of newspaper accounts, period household items, several interactive displays and life-size dioramas," *The Times of Northwest Indiana* reporter Andrew Steele wrote. "It tracks in detail Dillinger's years as one of America's most notorious criminals."

It attracted rave reviews. The museum captured Dillinger's hardship and concrete details of his life, like the lucky rabbit's foot he gave away months before his death. Terry Turner wrote in the *Sioux City Journal*:

> For those who want to find out what it was like for Dillinger when he spent 8½ years in a jail cell the museum has a replica of that small confinement space. His stay in jail apparently did little to deter him in a life of crime. Almost immediately after his release on May 10, 1933, Dillinger robbed

a bank in Bluffton, Ohio. He was captured a few months later and sent to the jail in Lima, Ohio. Friends of his who had escaped from the Indiana State Prison broke Dillinger out of that jail but in the process killed the sheriff making the whole gang accessories to murder. On John Dillinger's 31st birthday FBI director J. Edgar Hoover made the notorious criminal Public Enemy No. 1.

South Shore Convention and Visitors Authority officials considered repurposing the space the museum occupied as a Starbucks or a museum incubator. It briefly offered visitors decamping from the Borman Expressway free popcorn and pop at a fountain machine and ended up being used mainly to expand the gift shop, especially with *A Christmas Story* merchandise that was heavily promoted during the Indiana Welcome Center's popular *A Christmas Story Comes Home* exhibit. Despite being a top tourist attraction along the South Shore, the museum was relocated in 2015 to the basement of the Old Courthouse in downtown Crown Point, where it abruptly closed in August 2017. It was later replaced by Core Crown Point, a gym that specialized in Pilates, yoga, cycling, Bodhi suspension and other group exercises.

EPILOGUE

Hammond is a city that appreciates its history.

The Hammond Historical Society has worked for decades to preserve memories of the city's glory days. It hosts historical presentations about once a month, has published many books recording Hammond at various points in its history, collaborates with the Suzanne G. Long Local History Room at the Hammond Public Library on maintaining a robust archive, hosts special events like a commemoration of the Standard Steel Company strike massacre victims and leads the curious on its annual Suzanne G. Long Memorial Cemetery Tour of the Oak Hill Cemetery. It's an information-rich tour in which visitors can learn about bygone vaudeville performers, business magnates and other prominent figures of Hammond's early days.

Hammond is also a city that writes over its history like a palimpsest. Take the River Park Apartments on the banks of the Little Calumet River that were long sullied by crime and blight until Mayor Thomas McDermott Jr. tore them down. The troubled apartment complex has since been replaced with the Oxbow Landing development that includes office buildings, hotels, a Buffalo Wild Wings and Byway Brewing, which won best brewery in the state five months after it opened in 2016. You can't quite see the Little Cal from the patio at Byway, but you can sip a ChiPA India Pale Ale there while savoring chilled shrimp gazpacho or the "Khalil Mac" spin on the Big Mac.

Old-timers and others might claim Hammond isn't what it used to be. Downtown department stores and movie palaces no longer draw throngs of

Epilogue

Left: Hermann Gurfinkel's *Man of Steel* sculpture looms over Harrison Park just south of downtown Hammond. *Hammond Public Library.*

Below: The Hammond Marina opened the city's lakeshore up to boaters. *Hammond Public Library.*

Epilogue

La Vendor Cigar Company is one of the many long-gone Hammond factories. *Hammond Public Library.*

Epilogue

Hammond has been a manufacturing hub for companies like the Commercial Wallpaper Company. *Hammond Public Library.*

residents. The Woodmar Mall, itself a usurper, no longer packs them in to sit on Santa's lap. There are no longer Ferris wheels, perch palaces and roller-skating rinks that were pure magic every weekend; 3 Floyds came and went. But the city maintains a vitality even in a post-industrial age in which the Rust Belt is routinely dismissed along with the rest of "flyover country." On the weekends, traffic backs up down Indianapolis Boulevard to get into the Walmart right by the Chicago border and the Hammond Horseshoe Casino, the biggest casino in Chicagoland and the state of Indiana. The Horseshoe Casino proves to be a big draw year-round, drawing countless Chicagoans across the border. Beyond the gaming, it boasts the Venue, which has hosted acts like Steve Martin and Martin Short, Boyz II Men and four-time Grammy Award–winning India Arie and the Wine Spectator Award–winning Jack Binion Steakhouse with sweeping views of Lake Michigan that the *Chicago Tribune* described as "an upscale experience rivaling downtown's finest steakhouses." New and varied restaurants like Tzatziki Greek Street Food, Street Shack, Frankie V's and the Emerald Green at Lost Marsh routinely open across the city. Purdue University Northwest, the state's fifth-largest college after the consolidation between Purdue Calumet in Hammond and Purdue Northwest in Westfield, continues to make a splash and invest in storefronts along Indianapolis Boulevard.

Epilogue

Hammond has remained a manufacturing town ever since Lake George Ice started harvesting ice cubes in the city. *Hammond Public Library.*

The Gibson Woods are one of Hammond's major natural attractions. *Photo by author.*

Epilogue

An old industrial city bordering Chicago on the inland ocean of Lake Michigan that's been an occasional center of labor strife, the city is filled with factories but also resplendent with natural beauty. Hammond is home to more than 950 acres of city parks, including the Hammond Marina and the 129-acre Gibson Woods Nature Preserve, home to a beautiful flower-strewn pond during the spring. The city's also home to cultural resources like the Challenger Learning Center and Planetarium, the Hammond Environmental Education Center, the Indiana Welcome Center's W.F. Wellman Exhibit Hall, the South Shore Art League Station #2 gallery and the SideCar Gallery, which an Art Institute of Chicago employee runs out of a sidecar house next to his home. It hosts dynamic events like the Region Riot Criterium, the WHAM after-midnight bike ride and the Region-wide annual 219 Day celebration at the Hammond Civic Center.

A melting pot for many immigrants and ethnicities, the city once had more than 110,000 residents but has been declining in population since 1970. Hammond, however, remains the largest city in Lake County, which ranks second statewide in population with nearly 500,000 residents. The city is still home to about 80,000 residents and remains vital and diverse. One can wash down a one-pound BLT with an IPA at Flat Rock Tap or wolf down a banh mi at Asian Kitchen. You can see Billboard Chart-topping musicians at the Wolf Lake Pavilion or the underground Southeast Side Chicago rapper CoJack at 18th Street Brewing downtown. Hammond many no longer have the glitzy theaters or gaudy department stores of yesteryear, or the idyllic suburban shopping at Woodmar Mall, but it's retained a lot of retail, much of its industry and stately homes. Its unemployment and crime rates remain much lower than its neighbors in North Lake County, and in 2019, it didn't have a single homicide until July 4, tying a record set in the early 1980s. The city remains forward-thinking with its College Bound program, efforts to expand its municipal water utility and the glistening new Hammond SportsPlex for youth travel sports leagues. Hammond is a city with a rich history and a real future.

Much of Hammond has indeed been lost. Much of the past has faded or rusted away. Businesses have shuttered, buildings razed and memories vanished into the ether. But the Rust Belt city on the sandy cusp of Lake Michigan—the longtime font of soap, steel and Sloppy Joe–like loose meat burgers served at vintage lunch counters—soldiers on to the future, day in and day out, like a steel-toed-boot-wearing factory worker with all pluck and no quit. Hammond is a city that clocks in. It's a city that has not yet clocked out.

BIBLIOGRAPHY

Ball, T.H. *Lake County, Indiana, from 1834 to 1872*. Chicago: J.W. Goodspeed, 1873.

———. *Northwest Indiana from 1800 to 1900, or A View of our Region Through the Nineteenth Century*. Chicago: Donohue & Henneberry, 1900.

Cannon, Thomas Harvey. *History of the Lake and Calumet Region of Indiana Embracing the Counties of Lake, Porter and LaPorte*. Washington, D.C.: Historians' Association, 1927.

Dorson, Richard. *Land of the Millrats*. Cambridge, MA: Harvard University Press, 1981.

Eck, Kimberly, and Jennifer Linko. *Whiting and Robertsdale*. Charleston, SC: Arcadia Publishing, 2013.

Federal Writers Project. *Calumet Region Historical Guide*. Seattle, WA: Amazon Digital Services, 2014.

Funk, Terry, and Scott E. Williams. *More Than Just Hardcore*. Champaign, IL: Sports Publishing, 2005.

Hayward, Edward B. *Pages from the Past*. Hammond: Perspectives of the Calumet Region, 1991.

Lane, James. *Age of Anxiety: Daily Life in the Calumet Region during the Postwar Years, 1945–1953*. Gary: Indiana University Northwest, 2003.

———. *Home Front: The World War II Years in the Calumet Region, 1941–1945*. Gary: Indiana University Northwest, 1993.

———. *Life in the Calumet Region During the 1970s*. Gary: Indiana University Northwest, 1983.

Bibliography

———. *Life in the Calumet Region During the Year 2000.* Gary: Indiana University Northwest, 2002.

———. *The Postwar Period in the Calumet Region, 1945–1950.* Gary: Indiana University Northwest, 1988.

Letica, John. *Totin' Ties in the Harbor.* Gary: Indiana University Northwest, 1988.

McKinlay, Archibald. *Chicago's Neighboring South Shore: Lake County, Indiana.* Virginia Beach, VA: Donning Co. Publishers, 2001.

———. *Reejin Archetypes.* Chicago: Cattails Press, 1996.

Moore, Powell A. *The Calumet Region: Indiana's Last Frontier.* Indianapolis: Indiana Historical Bureau, 1959.

Schoon, Kenneth J. *Calumet Beginnings: Ancient Shorelines and Settlements at the South End of Lake Michigan.* Bloomington: Indiana University Press, 2003.

Singer, Leslie P. *The American Middle-Sized City: Hammond, Indiana.* Bloomington: Indiana Office of Manpower Development and Urban Institute, School of Public and Environmental Affairs, Indiana University, 1978.

Skertic, Mark. *A Native's Guide to Northwest Indiana.* Chicago: Lake Claremont Press, 2003.

Taylor, Troy. *Blood, Guns & Valentines.* Decatur, IL: Whitechapel Productions, 2010.

Trusty, Lance. *Hammond: A Centennial Portrait.* Norfolk, VA: Donning Co., 1984.

Weitgenant, Ann. *Lake County Heritage.* Dallas, TX: Curtis Media Corp, 1990.

Whitney, Gordon D. *History of the Hammond Fire Department.* Hammond, IN: Hammond Historical Society, 1978.

Woods, Sam B. *The First Hundred Years of Lake County, Indiana.* Crown Point, IN: self-published, 1938.

INDEX

A

Aristotle of the Airwaves 153

B

Borman Expressway 17, 61, 115, 178, 183, 186, 191
Bulger, Whitey 179, 180

C

Calumet City 15, 25, 38, 48, 50, 51, 67, 71, 94, 105, 107, 116, 162, 171
Capone, Al 38, 48, 49, 84, 105, 175, 176
Cavalier Inn 153
Chicago 11, 12, 13, 15, 16, 17, 19, 22, 23, 25, 30, 32, 34, 35, 37, 38, 41, 44, 46, 48, 50, 51, 52, 54, 55, 56, 58, 61, 63, 67, 71, 73, 74, 77, 81, 82, 83, 91, 95, 96, 98, 100, 104, 107, 109, 111, 114, 117, 118, 120, 127, 128, 129, 138, 140, 141, 143, 144, 146, 148, 149, 150, 152, 153, 154, 155, 160, 163, 166, 167, 170, 171, 174, 175, 176, 177, 179, 181, 189, 196, 198, 205
Chicago Outfit 38, 112, 171
Christmas Story, A 11, 61, 98, 100, 103, 154, 191
Clark, Dick 87
Conkey Street 122, 129

INDEX

D

Dedelow, Jim 152
Depp, Johnny 179
Dillinger, John 84, 189, 191

E

Earhart, Amelia 108
East Chicago 16, 58, 74, 75, 149, 150, 154
E.C. Minas 11, 90
18th Street Brewery 75, 119, 177
El Taco Real 19

F

First Baptist Church of Hammond 71, 72, 75, 95
Five Points 11, 52, 54, 55, 56, 57, 58, 61, 62, 74

G

Gary, Indiana 11, 15, 16, 17, 23, 30, 58, 61, 70, 72, 80, 83, 94, 100, 155, 168, 177, 190
Goldblatt's 67, 72, 75, 94, 98, 100, 101, 103
Gompers, Samuel 123
Grand Hotel LaSalle 105, 107

H

Hammond Distilling 174
Hammond, George 13, 14, 28, 30, 31
Hammond Pros 166, 168
Hammond Public Library 83, 84, 94, 103, 120, 181, 193, 205
Hessville 19, 27, 89, 182, 188
Hohman 13, 14, 19, 21, 27, 52, 66, 72, 73, 74, 75, 77, 81, 87, 90, 93, 96, 98, 103, 104, 105, 106, 109, 119, 121, 131, 140, 143, 152
Hohman Avenue 14, 19, 27, 66, 72, 73, 74, 75, 77, 81, 87, 96, 98, 105, 106, 109, 119, 131, 143, 152
Hope, Bob 87, 110

I

Indiana Botanical Gardens 184
Indianapolis 500 45, 46

K

King Bee Roller Coaster 56

L

Lake Michigan 12, 14, 15, 19, 30, 35, 52, 57, 58, 61, 62, 111, 114, 120, 147, 196, 198
lake perch 35, 46, 52, 110, 114, 115, 116, 117
Leopold and Loeb 38, 39

INDEX

M

Madura's Danceland 54, 55, 56
Maravilla, Karen 75
McDermott, Thomas, Jr. 108, 145, 150, 193
McKinlay, Archibald 17, 54, 57, 58, 118, 139, 141, 143, 144, 149, 181, 184
Miner-Dunn 117, 118

N

National Football League 11, 166, 167
Nelson, Baby Face 45
Nine Span Bridge 149, 150, 151
NIPSCO 72, 73, 113

O

Oak Hill Cemetery 143, 193

P

Paramount Theatre 11, 77, 85, 87, 88, 176
Parthenon Theatre 11, 77, 78, 80, 85, 87
Paul Henry's 22, 23, 75
Pence, Mike 190
Phil Smidt's 11, 52, 110, 112, 114, 115, 116
Polish Cavalcade of Music 153
Purdue Calumet University 161

R

railroad 17, 29, 31, 40, 56, 61, 74, 105, 106, 120, 121, 122, 124, 125, 149
Rinso 61, 62, 63, 65
Robertsdale 17, 35, 41, 52, 55, 56, 62
Roby 41, 43, 44, 45, 46, 47, 52, 58
Roebuck, Alvah Curtis 11, 138, 139

S

Sears 11, 100, 131, 138, 139, 140, 141
Shedd Aquarium 13, 41, 148
Shepherd, Jean 11, 46, 75, 86, 98, 100, 102, 103, 104, 154
Sinatra, Frank 110
South Shore Line 25, 54, 55, 73, 76, 121, 149
Standard Oil 53, 115, 131, 151
State Line Slaughterhouse 14, 27, 28, 31
Strack & Van Til 75, 107, 185
Straube Piano Company 143

T

Taylor Chain Company 127, 128
Towle 13, 19, 30, 75, 81, 90, 174, 205

U

Unilever 61, 64, 65, 110

V

Vogel's 117

W

W.B. Conkey 14, 15, 129, 131, 132, 134, 138
Whiting 15, 16, 17, 19, 41, 43, 44, 47, 52, 55, 57, 67, 74, 75, 77, 110, 169
WJOB 102, 103, 152, 154, 155, 205
Wolf Lake 12, 19, 27, 35, 37, 38, 39, 40, 53, 58, 110, 198, 205
Wooden, John 169
Woodmar Country Club 157, 159
Woodmar Mall 11, 71, 94, 103, 160, 164, 196, 198

ABOUT THE AUTHOR

Region native Joseph S. Pete was born in downtown Hammond and lived just outside the city for much of his life. He is an award-winning journalist, an Iraq War veteran, an Indiana University graduate, a book reviewer, a photographer, the editor-in-chief of the *Northwest Indiana Literary Journal*, a staff writer and Sunday columnist for *The Times of Northwest Indiana* and a frequent guest on Lakeshore Public Radio. He is a Pushcart Prize and Best of the Net nominee whose writing and photography have appeared in more than 150 literary journals, including *Spirits, Dogzplot, Stoneboat, The High Window, Synesthesia Literary Journal, Steep Street Journal, Beautiful Losers, New Pop Lit, The Grief Diaries, Gravel, The Offbeat, Oddball Magazine, The Perch Magazine, Rising Phoenix Review, Chicago Literati* and *McSweeney's Internet Tendency.* He has appeared on WGN Radio, WJOB and Lakeshore Public Television. His writing has been featured in several books, including *Indiana at 200, Poets to Come: Walt Whitman's Bicentennial, Words and Other Wild Things* and *Sex, Drugs and Copenhagen.* You can often find him at the Hammond Public Library, the Towle Theatre, Wolf Lake, 18th Street or Byway Brewing, and he's been known to crush the one-pound BLT at Flat Rock Tap from time to time. He never misses Festival of the Lakes and remembers when it was called August Fest.

Visit us at
www.historypress.com

www.ingramcontent.com/pod-product-compliance
Lightning Source LLC
Chambersburg PA
CBHW040303170426
43194CB00021B/2877